Whoever You Are

Margarida • Liz • Jean

Three ordinary women – Three stories of an amazing God

Published by WEC Publications,
Bulstrode, Gerrards Cross, Bucks. SL9 8SZ, England

ISBN 0 900828 84 6

Cover by Sam Richardson

Whoever You Are

Margarida • Liz • Jean

Three ordinary women – Three stories of an amazing God

Whoever You Are

Three inspirational true stories…

Margarida was an autistic girl from a Brazilian slum; now she teaches at a Bible college in Africa.

Liz is an Australian nurse who became a friend of drug addicts, and started a church in the kitchen of a Dutch brothel.

Jean was a middle-aged divorcee from England who exercised a healing and prayer ministry in Afghanistan amid the bombs and rockets of the invading Taliban.

Three ordinary women. Three stories of amazing grace… for anyone who has ever thought, I can't.

Contents

Margarida

Favelada - a slum kid

A broken doll

My family says that I was a very strange girl. It's true. And this is my story.

Like many squatters, the poor and the destitute, my family lived on the mountainside on the edge of Rio de Janeiro. Multitudinous stairs, irregular and difficult to manage, led to our long frame house which was built into the mountainside and was supported at the front by sixteen-foot-high wooden pillars. Once it may have been a one-family house but it had been divided into a row of single-room dwellings, one of which was rented by my parents and another by my mother's sister, Aunt Nega, and her family.

It was vacation time, 1961, so Aunt Nega's children were home from the government boarding school. My older cousins, a brother and sister, were playing with me, their two-year-old 'doll'. Dolls are often neglected as the 'grown-ups' play. But their 'doll' did not stay put. A normal, active, curious child, I climbed on to the bed to look out the window. I could look wa-a-a-y down to the ground and even further down to the huge reservoir. Leaning over to see, I suddenly fell crashing down twenty feet onto the rough cement in front of the reservoir. Too shocked to utter a sound, I was discovered by my brother Antonio and the others when they heard the crash. Screaming, they ran out of the house, down the stairs and through the gate to the reservoir.

'Is she dead?' asked my cousin Ana, who at ten was the oldest girl in the group. Antonio already had me in his arms. No answer was needed as I started to cry. Bija (my baby-talk for Luiza, my six year old sister) threw herself on to me and howled. Lovingly, Antonio carried me up the stairs and into the house.

'Bring a wet cloth,' my worried and guilt-ridden brother instructed. 'Her head is bleeding.'

My cousin Lucas was quick to do what he could. For three hours Antonio held me, his beloved baby sister, rocking me, trying to comfort me, trying to give me a drink of water or food, while all I did was scream. Ana had seen her mother treat open wounds and followed her example. She grabbed the salt jar and poured some on a cloth which she applied to my head. That didn't stop the bleeding.

'Get the coffee,' Lucas suggested, 'and put some on the cloth.' Eagerly Ana followed the instructions for the home remedy.

'What's the matter?' my Aunt Nega asked as she entered the house. She picked up the screaming toddler, who was obviously in great pain. As she paced the floor, lovingly patting me, the others filled her in with the details.

'Will she live?' asked Bija.

'Yes, yes,' Nega said hopefully, 'She'll be all right.'

Little did any of them guess the extent of the emotional pain that would plague me for fifteen torturous years, or the physical problems which I suffered as a result.

Poverty trap

As a young man my grandfather had left his home and family in the interior of the state of Minas Gerais to make his fortune. Being illiterate and there being no telephones he never again contacted his family, so when his father died the estate (which was considerable) was divided between his brothers and sisters. They hadn't heard from him for years and didn't know whether he was alive or not.

My grandfather and his family all panned for gold in a nearby river. They had plenty of food and money for clothes and other necessities, but had no savings and never owned property. He sold the gold they panned to the first bidder, never holding out for a better price. The money he got he squandered on drink and gambling. Easy come, easy go! It seems that he had made some sort of pact with the devil for prosperity, which resulted in poverty. His god was money, his goal in life was to be rich. Although Catholic in name, he didn't practice his religion though his wife did.

He died of cancer, hastened by an accident caused by a daring stunt, and left his widow destitute with four children – an eighteen-year-old boy, a fourteen-year-old girl (Maria, my mother) and two younger girls. The son died young and my grandmother and her daughters lived in abject poverty.

In 1948, when my grandmother was living in a small town with two of her three daughters, an abandoned infant, Antonio, was placed in her care. This devoted Catholic lady saw the child as coming from God and took him into her heart and home.

My grandmother and her family moved to Rio de Janeiro in search of a better life. They had not been there long when my grandmother died and my mother inherited Antonio who was just three years old. My mother worked in a factory for thirteen years during which time she married a seemingly respectable, sociable, hard-working docker, twelve years her junior. My father accepted Antonio as his own. In the next seven years my mother had six pregnancies but only Luiza (Bija) and I survived. How glad she was to have Antonio, a loving, thoughtful lad.

Later, my mother worked as a maid in wealthy homes, but even so, we still lived in the slums. Father wasted his earnings on alcohol, tobacco and the carnival. He became a different person when drunk. He had neither money nor concern for his family, not even for his wife during her six pregnancies. Any nice things given to my mother or bought with her earnings he deliberately destroyed. When she bought good food he always took the best. One Christmas, when my sister and I were earning money, we bought a turkey, a chicken, a leg of pork, nuts and everything needed to make a feast. Father came in drunk and threw everything on the floor, trampling it underfoot. We couldn't eat any of it.

For thirty-one years Mother endured his drunkenness, swearing, smoking (three packs of twenty a day), his total lack of affection and the enforced poverty. Although she never deserted him, he sometimes disappeared for the weekend. He gave financial help only sporadically, leaving Mother to raise the family in poverty.

The death of my brother

When he was twelve years old, Antonio found work at the Thursday Market. He was a joy to his family, dependable, responsible and loving. What a comfort he was to my mother!

One day, just a month after my fall, he was returning home, tired but happy, with some bags of produce and a few coins in his pocket. As he crossed the busy street in front of a bus, a speeding car hit him but kept going and disappeared. The police came and while one took testimonies from witnesses, including description and license plate of the car, another took the unconscious boy to the hospital. In God's providence, one of the witnesses knew Antonio and hurried to report the accident to my mother.

Overcome with grief, my mother cried hysterically at the sight of her beloved son lying in the hospital in a coma, with internal as well as external injuries. The hospital staff gently led her away and registered her into a ward.

Poor Father! Five days later his son was still in a coma. His wife, broken with grief to the point of hysteria, was sedated in the same hospital and I was at home suffering from my fall a month before. Bija, at six years old, was not much help either, just another burden. Turning to the only solace he knew, the lanky dockworker entered the bar. Fortunately, Aunt Nega was in the house to care for us.

The doctors could not revive Antonio. Five days later, he died. Shock and grief overwhelmed my mother. She had already lost two infants and suffered two miscarriages. Now her beloved, only son was gone. What about me? Was she about to lose me too?

My tragedy intensifies

It wasn't only my parents who grieved over the loss of their son. I had loved my brother dearly. His death, so soon after my fall, coupled with my mother's absence while she was in hospital, added to the trauma. My personality changed and I went from bad to worse.

A month after my fall my mother decided she must take me to see a doctor. 'Doctor,' she told him, 'my baby was happy and active. She ran around and jabbered all the time. Now look at her – she just lies there, quiet and sad. I'm the only one she responds to. She doesn't want to walk, she doesn't talk. What can I do?'

After examining me and hearing the story of my fall, he referred me to a bone specialist who concluded that nothing was broken. It was decided that my problem was mental and I was referred to a psychiatrist.

The psychiatrist was very kind to me. She treated me with medication, games and conversation. But I couldn't respond to the games or to the conversations. A few years later she was replaced by a man I could not relate to at all. I didn't like him and I got worse. Repeated EEGs (electroencephalograms) indicated brain abnormalities. My psychiatrist gave me medicines but they only exacerbated the problem. I withdrew into my own world and suffered abuse from all but my mother. I couldn't relate to people and my emotions seemed to have died. My mother was alarmed by my change of behaviour. As I grew up, I had no friends in the neighbourhood. My relationship with Bija was minimal and even with my mother it was abnormally limited. Because of my compulsion to repeat apparently meaningless motions, my limited response and my lack of emotion, a psychiatrist later told me that I had all the signs of autism.

Problems continued at home. 'You're crazy,' Bija jeered, as she tormented me, pulling at my legs and punching me. 'There you are, lying on your back with your feet propped up high on the wall. You don't do anything. You just lie there and stare.' I continued to stare at the ceiling and walls. I saw things no one else saw: people, animals, houses and food. 'What are you laughing about?' asked the annoyed Bija as she vigorously swept the floor. 'I heard you when I was outside saying things that don't mean anything.'

I talked to my mother about this. As she was the only one I could relate to, I wanted her to stay in the house with me all the time. I had no relationship with my father. While I was too young to know what it meant, he raped me many times. My autism made me unable to tell anyone. I did not discover exactly what he had done until years later when I had a medical examination at Bible school, but I knew it was dreadful. I didn't talk to him until I was a teenager. Then I was very rude to him.

'Minito' (my pronunciation for Bonito), my beautiful little dog, never taunted me. I would hold him tightly under my arm and chew on his ears. He accepted me and seemed to understand me.

I had an obsessive compulsion to repeat simple actions such as pacing back and forth but going nowhere, or sitting on Mother's lap twisting her ear over and over by the hour. I cried and cried if I was alone, yet I created my own world where I could stay for days at a time. Sometimes I could not bear any exterior stimuli. I would hit my head on the wall, or start to walk from one side of the room to the other. At other times, when people bothered me, I screamed or started doing things they didn't understand. Sometimes I would stare at people or things for a long time without moving.

Once when our landlords, Aparacida and Josefa, came to collect the rent I gave them a blank stare out of the top of my eyes and ran into the house. Mother stepped out of the house and invited them in. I hid behind her, head down but staring at the visitors. 'What's the matter with her?' Aparacida asked. 'I've never seen a child look at me like that. She's peering at me out of the top of her eyes like she's looking up over reading glasses.' She turned to me, 'Can't you hold your head up and look right at me?' I darted away to the bed in the corner and crawled under it. 'Look she's hiding. She thinks we can't see her under there. What a queer child she is!'

Another time a more understanding neighbour came with a dish full of sweets. 'Here, Margarida, would you like some sweets?' she asked. I shrugged my shoulders, grabbed some, ran away and wrapped myself up in an old wool blanket. 'Child, get out of there!' she exclaimed.' It's so hot today, you'll suffocate.' But the blanket was protection from my enemies, the people looking at me.

When I was six I attended school briefly, but left because I could not socialise. The excuse was that I was too sick to go to school, the doctor's prescriptions being used as evidence. And there was other evidence. When people talked to me I could not answer. It seemed that there was a wall between other people and me. I heard and understood everything but could not respond. Laughing or shouting was my only communication.

I had three speech therapists. When I first went to school, one of them really tried to help me. She would talk to me and teach me how to pronounce words that I didn't know. Pronunciation was one of my problems for a long time. Even when I was in university I did a course on pronunciation.

I was almost ten when I next went to school. My teacher, Dona Diva, was very kind to me and even helped me take my medicines. I think it was because of her that I didn't leave school again.

At eleven, I was enrolled in another school and placed with children aged eight and nine. I was the oldest, the tallest and the quietest. Since I did not talk the children assumed I could not hear or understand either. 'You're dumb!' 'You're crazy!' 'You don't know anything.' These were some of the hurtful remarks I heard over and over again. Inwardly I cried. I hated those kids, and with chin down and eyeballs raised, I silently stared them down.

'See that boy,' I confided in Bija. 'He smacked me today.' And another day, 'He pulled my braids.' Love for her little sister and anger against my tormentors triggered many a fight. At times she would take on the harasser alone; at other times it would turn into a multi-family brawl. Bija was always there to protect me. She always wanted to back up her love with hugs and kisses. Inside I loved her but was unable to express it. I just stiffened up.

I had no friends at school. The teachers didn't seem to notice that I was handing in acceptable papers, except one kind and understanding teacher who helped me pass three grades in one year. Bija also helped me at home, so I could read, count and do simple calculations.

My mother turns to spiritism

My mother always loved me. Although she could not read, she had learnt the stories of the saints and how to gain their favour. Deeply concerned about my psychological problems, she felt she needed the help of Saint Cosme and Saint Damiao, twin doctors who had been canonised and were said to help children with problems. She went to the church of Saint Cosme and Saint Damiao and took them a symbolic sacrifice – a wax head which was intended to release the problems in my mind. My mother made a vow to honour their special day, September 27th, by giving treats to the neighbourhood children for seven years in a row. It meant financial hardship but she did it for three years, even though she knew this custom stemmed from spiritism. She was concerned only about my healing. (In Brazilian culture African spiritism has blended with Catholicism over the centuries and the same saints are contacted and worshipped in both.)

Next my mother made a seven-year vow to St. Sebastian, the

keeper of our city, Rio de Janeiro. Each year for seven years she sewed special clothes for me – a short red dress with a shoulder band across the front. She placed a lighted candle, which was as tall as I was, in my hand. In January, the hottest month of the year, we had to walk in procession some 32 kilometres to St. Sebastian's church. My mother wore sandals but I had to do that tortuous walk barefoot. It was usually at least 40°C or more. My feet blistered but I took it as a punishment my mother was inflicting on me. I felt she was being cruel to me. I hated it and I hated the Catholic Church. It held only bad memories for me. Every Sunday we went to Mass but to me it was all a blank, even though the services were conducted in Portuguese.

Ever seeking a miraculous healing my mother made another vow, to Our Lady of Penha (Rock). Her splendid, magnificent church was on a high rock with 365 steps leading to it. To receive a miracle from her, my mother vowed to crawl up those steps on her knees. Year after year my mother did this with Bija and me walking alongside her. I didn't understand that it was for me that she was blistering her knees in the hot sun. When we arrived home from that church I had to take medicines to calm my agitated nerves. I was so tired from going up those 365 stairs that when we were dragging ourselves up the hill to our home, I got out of control. I remember that I broke two cups, and started to hit my head against the wall.

Mum bought an icon of the Infant Jesus of Prague (*Menino Jesus de Praga*) because she had heard that he had done many miracles as a child. This icon was supposed to do a miracle for me but all she ever received was disillusionment and frustration. She had never known any other child with my problems. It took years for her to realise that I had an unusual emotional problem. She watched me stiffen up and turn away when guests wanted to talk to me. She wondered why I didn't want to relate to other people.

Bija turns to drugs

Bija also gave her problems.

'I gave my bracelet to Floriceia,' Bija complained to my mother, 'and now she won't give it back to me.'

'Where did you get the bracelet from, anyway?' my mother asked.

'I borrowed it and now the owner wants it back,' replied Bija. 'I'll go and talk to Floriceia about it,' declared my mother. When Floriceia denied having it my mother went to her mother, Vilma.

'My girl didn't steal anything!' insisted Vilma. 'Go to the spiritists to find out where the bracelet is.'

The bracelet had been stolen and my mother was being given the run-around. Finally, she resorted to a spiritist. She got no help there as the spiritist told lies. Mum discovered that Vilma was seeing the same spiritist with the intention of harming our family.

Bija was a clever girl. She helped in the home and although she did well in school, the school was not so good for her. In the playground she was offered marijuana and began smoking it. Why not? Mother and Father both smoked a lot. She decided to try it and thought it was fun. It was easy to get as she helped the dealer and he gave her the stuff. She started with small amounts, using it only around the school, never at home. After a couple of years Bija started to smoke it when we were out. I knew what she was doing and knew it was wrong, but in my little psychological cage I kept everything to myself.

Once when my mother was washing clothes at the public washbasins she overheard the women gossiping. Vilma, our neighbour, started to criticise Bija.

'She's just a no-good drug addict. That's all she is.'

'She is not!' defended my mother.

'Oh yes she is. She smokes marijuana, sniffs cocaine and sleeps with dealers.'

'I don't see any evidence of it. You're a liar!'

But when she got home she confronted Bija. Tearfully Bija admitted it. 'I didn't tell you because I didn't want you to know. I've been doing it for four years now.' Together they cried; my mother cried because her daughter was a drug addict, my sister cried because our mother had found out. Bija was nearly fifteen and from that time on my father required me to accompany her and to watch her when she went out at night. She delighted in parties and dancing but I never participated in the activities.

'Everything's okay,' I would report, not that I knew because while she was dancing I was sleeping. Even at the School of Samba (a weekly rehearsal for the annual four-day carnival) I would look for a place to sleep. While Bija joined the crowds gathered for entertainment, drinking and socialising, I escaped from reality.

'When I'm ready to go home, I'll call you.' Bija said. She knew where to look for me. I slept for hours sitting on the toilet.

Light shines in the darkness

Mother finds the truth

My childhood had been plagued with problems: emotional, spiritual, physical, social and financial. The first release came in the spiritual realm, in my mother's life. This is her story:

'I was in church praying to the Virgin Mary, asking for Luisa's release from drug addiction. I genuflected before the main statue of Christ. "What can this statue do for me?" I wondered. "Nothing! He doesn't hear; he doesn't see. What can he do for me?"

'Desperate, I left and returned to the spiritists. I talked with them but soon realised the devil couldn't give me anything, either. Even more desperate, I started toward home. Walking up a path in the slum where I lived, I was drawn to a crowd gathered around a man who was shouting. I was amazed as I heard this man, a pastor, explaining the salvation that Jesus offered. I had never heard that before. My heart was ready; this was what I had been longing for. I met Christ. My problems were not solved, but inside I had joy and a song. My spirit was released!'

Just as I had been cut off from relationships with people, this fifty-eight year old illiterate housemaid had been cut off from a true relationship with God.

When it was time for her accustomed cigarette, she reached for a sweet instead and never smoked again. This was too good to keep to herself so she went to see Dona Vilma who was heavily involved with witchcraft. Little did my mother know that Vilma, whom she had looked upon as a friend, had done many things to destroy Bija.

'Vilma,' she called enthusiastically, 'this *macumba* (spiritism) is bad. It destroys people. Jesus Christ is the only way! The Lord Jesus really loves you. Come to the Evangelical Church with me!'

As my mother continued to hear preaching about Christ's salvation and deliverance, she repeatedly invited Vilma to church but was always rebuffed. Blinded and hardened by Satan, Vilma was determined to continue with her witchcraft but it didn't seem to work any more. She became nervous, lost her concentration and began speaking unintelligible things to herself. Finally Satan struck back. Her son was killed and she lost her sanity. Out of her mind, Vilma gathered her few belongings, tied them up in a sheet and set out on the street with her bundle on her head. Her children invited her into their homes, but she refused. She begged on the streets and on the streets she died. The evil she had perpetrated on others returned to her. Her daughter later confirmed that Vilma had put curses on Bija.

After my mother had attended the Evangelical Church for six months, Pastor Joao baptised her by immersion in a river. As God opened her eyes to the truth, she realised that more enlightenment was found in God's book, the Holy Bible. Never before had she needed to read it. The priest had warned her it was a dangerous book and that she should leave it alone. He would tell her what she needed to know. In the Evangelical Church people read the Bible and she wanted to read it too. Half a century before she had studied for just one year in a school several kilometres from her home. She still remembered the letters and Bija helped her over the hard places. In less than a year God enabled my fifty-nine-year-old mother to read.

The word of God is alive and powerful. She heard it in church and read it on her own. Alone in her own little one-room slum dwelling, God filled her with the Holy Spirit. She longed to work for her God and Saviour but saw no opportunity in the little independent church. Her untrained pastor lacked the skills needed to lead his congregation in ministry.

Early one morning, as my mother was praying, God spoke to her: 'To receive, you must lose.' Her church meant so much to her but God wanted her to leave it. God showed her a big old house with the sign 'Second Evangelical Church' on the front of it. She saw the building, the name of the street and the number. The next Sunday she asked Dad for the bus fare to go to this church. She had never seen the church but the Spirit of God led her to it and confirmed in her heart that this was the place.

Here again she heard the gospel and continued to hear about healing and deliverance from demonic activity. Later she began teaching the Bible to others. She had previously visited a prison with a group from another church but now she began visiting regularly with her own church.

Help for the Favelada

'Get her into sports,' the psychiatrist advised my mother. 'Take her to the university. They have a sports programme for needy children and you won't have to pay any fees.' And so it was that from age nine to nineteen I was trained in track and gymnastics. The goal was not only to develop my body but it was also hoped that I would relate to the other children. I learned quickly through instruction and observation and for a year I went to the university twice a week for an hour of instruction. Later, I trained as much as six hours a day in the nearby stadium.

For those ten years Coach Celbir stressed perfection and responsibility. Each manoeuvre had to be done precisely. We competed against our own records to reach our goals. I was glad that he didn't know my background and that he treated me just like the other children. We all enjoyed his loving humour. He demonstrated each manoeuvre and joined us in each exercise. He encouraged us and gently persisted until each child got it right.

Competitions were momentous for me. When I was fourteen I took first prize in the 200m race. The next year I took second prize in the 400m obstacle course and later, second place in a relay race.

It was again time for a competition and Celbir was scheduling extra practice but I had to tell him that I couldn't come to one of the sessions as I needed to go to the doctor. Because I looked healthy to him he was surprised and asked why. That was when I told him that I was seeing a psychiatrist every month and I told him about my past. When he learnt that I was taking Epilene and Gadernal he was concerned because those drugs were banned in competitions, yet he wanted me to compete. After consultation with the judges, I was permitted to enter the competition with a slight modification to my drug intake.

Celbir was also concerned about my speech impediment and asked when I last went to the dentist. I told him that I had only been to the school dentist who cleaned my teeth and told me that I wasn't brushing properly and ought to get a new toothbrush. But I never had the money to buy one. Celbir understood my financial situation and suggested that I went to the dental school at the university where I wouldn't have to pay. Fearfully I hesitated, but my swollen gums were red and painful and oozing blood, so I plucked up the courage to accept his recommendation.

At the University Dental Clinic, Dr. Valter examined and evaluated each new patient before assigning him or her to a student. He reported to the group of dental students that I didn't seem to have any cavities, but I did have problems with my gums and bone structure. After looking at x-rays of my mouth, he asked me, 'Did you have some sort of accident? What foods do you eat? How old are you? How old is your mother?' He wasn't certain of the cause of my problem but thought it might be related to some of these factors. He told his students that I was an unusual case and that they would treat me. I didn't like the idea of all those students studying me but it was the only way I could get help.

Over a twenty-year period Dr. Valter treated me many times, removing abscesses, scraping the bones, extracting teeth and fitting false ones. Now, my teeth are beautiful.

At seventeen, in spite of gymnastics and the care I received, I still continued in my emotional cage. I had made small improvements in relating to school teachers, my coach, my team-mates and the dentist, but not to others. When gym companions approached me for a conversation or activity I would respond but I never initiated conversation.

My conversion

'Here's another book for you Margarida, ' my mother said. 'Dona Silva sent it for you.' Eagerly I took the treasure sent by the lady my mother worked for. Another day she came home from work and saw me fascinated with an Old Testament story from her Bible. 'Do you want a Bible of your own?' she asked. I nodded my head but remained expressionless.

We had neither money nor celebration on my fourteenth birthday, but my mother promised that as soon as she had some money she would buy me a Bible of my own. At the end of the month she came home with the promised Bible. Although I was pleased, words still didn't come.

I was fascinated with the stories of Jesus. When I got to John 6:37 I read, '...whoever comes to me I will never drive away.' That grabbed my attention. I thought to myself, 'I'm always alone. Nobody accepts me. I have no friends but here the Bible says that God will accept me as I am.' I said in my heart, 'God, if you will accept me as I am I will accept You.'

Now I had a new friend, a new kind of friend and His name was JESUS! I could tell him everything. Never before had I been able to tell anyone what was troubling me. I started to change inside. Lying on my back with my legs propped up against the wall, I looked up to heaven and talked aloud to God. Yes, I could speak out loud to Him when I was alone. 'You see that person, you see that school. They say my hair is like steel wool. They say I'm black. They call me Favelada and retarded. But I'm not retarded. I can read better than they can and do my maths quicker than anyone. I understand all Dona Diva is teaching us.' If anyone invaded my privacy I continued expressing myself to Jesus silently.

While my mother was still attending her first church I accompanied her once or twice but I didn't like the people there. In fact I hated them because they wouldn't leave me alone. My mother had told them about my problems and asked them to pray for me. Pushy people wanted to put their hands on my head and pray over me but I didn't want them to touch me. 'You're demon possessed,' they shouted and tried to cast out the demons. They wanted to convert me. But I knew that I was already saved and not demon possessed. The preacher shouted the sermon but I wasn't deaf and I didn't like it. I did like reading the Bible, though, and it was a release to my spirit to have a friend in whom I could confide, to whom I could tell all my problems.

When my mother started to attend the second church I decided to accompany her. I tried it the first Sunday in September. It wasn't churchy, just a room at the rear of the property. The big house that God had shown my mother had been demolished and a new church was being built. I felt more comfortable there. My mother was new and hadn't told anyone my background so nobody pestered me. But it was still impossible for me to talk to strangers. I could only talk to my family. Although the preacher shouted, he made sense. He talked about baptism, which I knew about because I had read about it in the Bible.

'Dozens of believers are ready to be baptised. Does anyone

else want to be baptised?' he asked. I poked my mother, nodded and pointed to myself and she understood that I wanted to talk to the pastor. When the service ended I followed closely behind my mother as she took me to see him. I was glad my mother could talk for me.

'Margarida wants to be baptised,' she told the pastor.

'Do you know the Lord Jesus as your Saviour?' he asked me.

I nodded my head in reply. He hesitated because he didn't know me and wasn't sure that I was saved. With my head down and staring beyond him, I said, 'I was saved at the age of fourteen through reading the Bible.'

'Who is Jesus?' he questioned me.

'He is the Son of God who came to save people. He came to save me.'

'How do you know He saved you?'

'Because He died on the cross. I read it in the Bible.'

'At which moment were you saved?'

'When I read John's Gospel.'

'Did you kneel and ask Jesus to come into your heart?'

'No, I didn't. I said to Jesus that if he would accept me I would accept Him. That's all. I am a Christian and God has accepted me, so I want to be baptised.' Because of my answers, he agreed to baptise me.

A large crowd gathered at the river on Independence Day (September 7th). Forty or more people had been prepared for baptism including my cousin Lucas. The crowd bothered me because I didn't like to expose myself to so many people. I was relieved that we were not asked to give our testimonies but were just given straightforward questions that I could answer with a nod or a shake of my head. When I was baptised people shouted and cried, 'Glory to God!' I thought they were crazy. I didn't feel anything and had no reaction. I was only baptised because in the Bible God told me to.

Healed from autism

Two or three weeks later the pastor preached about healing. He spoke about the time when Jesus delivered many people who had been brought to him because they were demon-possessed. He told us how Jesus had driven out evil spirits with a word and healed all that were sick, fulfilling what the prophet Isaiah had said: 'He himself took our sicknesses and carried away our diseases' (Isaiah 53:4). I had seen it in the Bible but I hadn't applied it to myself.

'Jesus heals!' he said. 'He healed all our sicknesses and he can heal you too. If you are sick or want prayer you can come to the front.'

'You can be healed now,' my mother whispered to me.

'No, I don't like it. He would put his hand on my head.'

'You have to go,' she insisted. 'You need to be healed.'

'I will ask God to heal me, myself.'

When we got home I asked God to heal me, but instead of making an elaborate prayer I picked up all my medicine and said to God, 'You are going to heal me now because I want to be a normal person. I don't want to be like this.' Then I went outside and threw all my medicine in the ditch. I said to the Lord, 'I'm healed!' That's all I did, and by the grace of God I was healed from autism. When I told my mother that I had been healed she insisted that I still had to continue taking my medicine to keep me calm. Nothing more was said about it and my mother assumed that I was taking it as I had done for years.

A month passed. 'Here's the money you need for your medicine,' my mother said, handing me a stack of notes.

'No, Mother, I don't need it.'

'Why, have you still got some left? Where is it?'

'I dumped it all in the ditch the night after we heard that sermon about healing.'

'Oh no, Margarida!' my mother panicked. 'We must get you to the doctor.'

'I don't need to see the doctor any more,' I told her, 'or take any medicine because God has healed me.'

For years my nervous condition had been kept under control by medicine. In recent weeks I had remained calm and my mother was pleased with the way the medicine was working. But when she learned that I had not been taking it for a month, she insisted that we saw the doctor. In silence, we travelled by bus to the clinic.

The psychiatrist glanced at my chart and pondered. 'You must take the medicine,' he concluded.

'No, Doctor. God has healed me and I don't need medicine any more.'

Surprised that I was speaking normally, he gave me a long

hard look. 'All right, we'll observe you for a while and then maybe you can continue without it.'

My mother watched me and saw the change in me. I no longer needed to be alone. I no longer felt the compulsion to sleep. The nervousness was calmed and I stopped talking to myself. I could bear to stay with my father because the hatred had been taken away. I could accept people talking to me and I could see that they were interested in me. Gone was the depression that had led to fainting. When Bija imitated me I did not react as before.

After three months I had another EEG which showed my brain was normal. The doctor said that I didn't need to take any more medicine but he did advise me to see a psychologist. However, I didn't go because I didn't want to talk and talk. Jesus was better than any psychologist and I could talk to him. Even though I was healed it still took time for the cage I'd built around myself to crumble.

A place at university

Since I didn't begin my primary education until the age of eleven, it wasn't until I was twenty-one that I was ready for university. Some 120,000 applicants vied for the 6,000 places for the 1978 academic year. We had to take entrance exams on a series of successive Sundays from 7.30 a.m. to 1.00 p.m. Many who took the exams had prepared at private schools, but that cost money. Many were repeating them for the second or third time. What chance did I have?

The Lord had healed me to the extent that I was able to study with three other girls who had taken private classes to prepare for the examination. I helped them with chemistry and mathematics, pure science appealing to me more than people-based subjects such as history. They loaned me books and told me what to study. Each day as we finished our studies the conversation would turn to gossip and worldly affairs but as I had no interest in such things I used to leave at that point.

The exams were multiple choice and essay questions: ninety items for each of six major subjects and sixty items for the elective language test. What suspense we endured as we awaited the results in the newspaper! I felt I had done all right but was really amazed when I saw that I ranked number thirty-two! The reward was a four-year university education without tuition fees! I was elated. All that remained was for me to find the entrance fee.

'You've never given me anything,' I said to my father. 'All I ask you to pay is my registration fee. It's very important to me.' My father had no concept of the importance of education; he could not even sign his name and saw no reason to study. Mother was proud of me and sympathetic, but there was no way that we could afford it. I became depressed and almost desperate but I decided to work hard and earn the money to take the entrance exams again the next year. I was determined not to lose the opportunity to learn because of a lack of money.

My mother talked to many friends, asking to borrow money. I went to my pastor to ask for help, 'I don't have any money,' was his response. After all, why should he invest in me? I was just a black woman from the slums, and sort of strange. He had no hopes of my sticking it out. He thought that investing in me would be a waste of money. Father's sister could have helped but didn't. A friend at church suggested that I go to the University President to ask for exemption from the fees. I was reticent but she encouraged me to go. Father gave me a document stating his salary which I took to the police who then supplied me with an authorised document confirming the poverty of our family.

Apprehensively I entered the main office of the Federal University of Rio de Janeiro. I saw a sign indicating the President's office and outside, at a big desk, sat his secretary.

'Please may I see the President? I need to speak to him.'

'No, he's very busy,' was her curt reply. 'We're in the midst of registration and he has many things to attend to.' She returned to her typewriter. Disappointed beyond words, I dropped my head and stepped aside. Outwardly I wasn't crying, but inside, I was.

A well-dressed, grey-haired gentleman approached me. 'What's the problem young lady?' he asked.

'I must see the President and show him these papers. If I don't I can't register and today is the last day.'

He gently took the papers from my hand and scanned them. 'You are Margarida Virgilio? And you live at 1231 Leopoldo? Have you always lived there? Hmm. You did very, very well. And this is what you father earns? Is it just that you don't have the money today?'

'No, I've never had any money. We are very poor.'

'Step in here with me.' He led me into the University President's office and took his place behind the large desk. Addressing the three men seated across from him he said, 'Excuse me gentlemen, I have a little matter to take care of. It'll just take a moment.' Picking up the phone, he pressed a few buttons, 'Bete, take this name: Margarida Virgilio. Mark her down for complete exemption of fees... Yes... that's right. Give her the paper when she leaves my office... Yes. Much obliged.'

Turning again to me he said, 'I'm very impressed with your examination grades. You must keep your grades up and you must not fail any subjects.'

Smiling, I thanked him and hurried off to register. Tuition and registration fees were taken care of! I thanked God, and told Him that it was only His doing that I passed so well and that I was given exemption from the fees. I knew that it was a great thing that He had done for me.

Mother talked with a friend at church about me. Her son was a biology teacher and a college administrator. He helped me and gave me money to buy textbooks, but I still needed the money for bus fares, clothes, food and other necessities.

I had very few friends but during that first year in university God gave me a good friend, Ribeiro, who was blind. Being older than most of the students and having a sensitive nature, he understood me more than others did. When I told him about my problems he could understand my hurt, for he too had been unappreciated because of his handicap. He too had often been told 'You can't do that.' Mostly he saw my spirit but he wanted to know what I looked like so I gave him permission to touch my face.

'You've such long, fine hair and so many plaits. How many?'

'Maybe two hundred.'

'Your hair design is amazing, Margarida,' he told me. 'How do you find enough money to get that done?'

'I do it myself and I do it for others too.'

Ribeiro became my volunteer agent. I plaited hair for many of the girls, sometimes in the students' lounge, sometimes in their homes. Depending on the length of their hair and the design they wanted it took from forty minutes to as much as eight hours. They paid me well.

'Hey, I like this,' said Ribeiro when he felt my leather purse.
'Where did you get it?'

'I made it. I make them to sell.'

'Really? How much do you get for one?'

'Four thousand *cruzeiros*. But I have a hard time selling them.'
Ribeiro decided to help me with this too. He had no trouble
selling them. In fact he sold them faster than I could make them.

Although it was difficult for me to respond in lectures, God
enabled me and even helped me to give oral reports. My essays
were excellent but I had a problem with pronunciation because
I had not practised speech as normal children do. The first
month my Portuguese language teacher, Maria Helena, gave me
a low grade. I went to her office to explain about myself.

'Your essays are very good,' she told me. 'You've handed
them all in on time and received high grades in all of them. But
your class participation has been very limited and we have difficulty understanding you.'

When I showed her a document from the doctor her attitude
changed and she began to give me speech therapy. Patiently, she
drilled me until by the end of the university course I was 100%
better and my monthly grades had improved.

She started to call me Pearl and when I asked her why she
said, 'Margarida means a precious pearl or fragile flower that
needs care.' I was pleased to discover this.

My new sister

During carnival time in 1974 Bija's friend Vanda came to see her.
She had a cigarette in one hand and her newborn baby in the
other. The two girls, aged nineteen and twenty, wanted to go to
the carnival. Vanda placed the four-day-old baby in my mother's arms and asked her to look after her for a while. Mother
looked at the beautiful little girl, dressed only in a little shirt and
nappy, with her umbilical cord still visible.

'What shall I give her?' my mother asked.

'Here's a bottle. That'll be enough. She doesn't need much,'
Vanda replied. We knew Vanda's reputation. She, a black junkie,
was married to Claudio, a white junkie. We knew her mother,
too, a hard woman. Janaina was Vanda's second baby; she had
allowed her first to die of neglect. At the carnival the girls
encountered a woman with whom Vanda had had some deal-

ings. They got into a fight and the woman threatened to shoot her. Vanda ran away and didn't come back.

Bija refused to take responsibility for her friend's child, saying, 'I didn't ask you to take this baby. She's nothing to do with me. She's your baby now.' Father bought a tin of powdered milk on credit and we tore up a sheet to make clothes for our 'doll'.

A month passed and there was still no sign of Vanda so we asked her mother to take the baby. 'No way!' she said. 'I brought up my own children but this baby isn't mine. No, I'm not going to look after her.'

So we contacted Claudio and asked what we should do with his baby daughter. 'I don't know where my wife is,' he responded. 'Will you keep her for a while? I'll give you money every month to feed her, clothe her and provide whatever she needs.' He loved his baby but was too busy with his drug trade to care for her.

Five months later Vanda arrived and asked my mother to keep the baby. But my mother refused, saying that she didn't have the money to take care of her. Vanda said that that wouldn't be a problem because Claudio would give us the money. Although he never paid us for full care of Janaina, he did give us some money every month and some groceries. But Claudio was killed by police in a drug raid when Janaina was only twenty months old. Vanda came occasionally to see her baby or take her for a walk.

When Janaina was two-and-a-half my mother decided that as she had no father and her mother didn't visit very often, we needed to talk to a judge about her. The judge took guardianship but gave the care of Janaina to my mother.

Ten years later Vanda decided that she wanted her daughter back so we had to go to court. 'I don't know her,' said Janaina pointing to Vanda. 'I don't have anything to do with her.'

Turning to my mother Janaina said, 'This is my mother and if she died I would not choose to live with Vanda but with my sisters, Bija and Margarida.' The judge awarded us custody of Janaina.

Vanda started visiting us again, saying that we had stolen her baby. One day she asked to take Janaina out and my mother gave her permission. Bija didn't trust Vanda and worried about why she wanted to take her out, so she went to Vanda's house to look for them. They were not there but when Vanda's family said that they had gone to the red light district, Bija became alarmed. Taking a taxi, she pursued them. Just as Bija feared, Vanda had taken the beautiful thirteen-year-old to a house of prostitution.

'I'm not going to stay here,' she heard her little sister scream. 'I want my mother!'

'You said that you were the mother,' said the pimp.

Bija pounded on the door. 'Give me my sister. You've stolen her. If you don't give her back now I'll call the police!'

The pimp, knowing that his slave trade was illegal, was afraid. 'Give her the girl,' he said to Vanda. 'Get out of here! You're nothing but trouble.'

Vanda came back again the next year, high on drugs and with a big knife, to wrest the potential source of income from the defenceless little old lady. But the healthy, drug-free fourteen-year-old overpowered her birth mother and forced her to leave.

Janaina has continued to be a blessing to my mother. She and her little daughter, Pamela, are constant companions for her and have always been there when she has needed support. Now that God has placed me in Guinea-Bissau it gives me a lot of peace to know that my eighty-five-year-old mother is being cared for in this way. We praise God for the unexpected blessing God gave us in that little abandoned baby.

Father's transformation

It was Janaina who coerced my father to go to church the Sunday he was saved.It was Fathers' Day, 12 August 1979.

'Father,' the five year old cajoled, 'You have to go to church with us today.'

'I do, do I? Who says so?'

'The pastor. All the fathers are going to church today and we have a present for all of them. The pastor said that anyone who came without a father would have to give their present to him. I don't want to give my present to him, I want to give it to you.'

'Well, that's just too bad. I'm not having any of that religious stuff.' After another smoke and a cup of coffee, he headed for the door.

'Father, you have to go to church with us.' Janaina was quite insistent, crying loudly and hanging onto the only man she had known as a father. Shaking her off, he headed for the bar where he tried to drown his conscience with booze. Sobbing, the little girl accompanied her mother to church. They joined others for special prayer for the fathers, then entered the sanctuary and sat in their accustomed pew near the front.

After my mother and Janaina had left, father came back home smelling strongly of alcohol. He reached for his good trousers and shirt, expensive new clothes which he had recently bought, and polished his shoes.

'Why are you dressing up, Father? Are you going to a party?' I asked.

'It's none of your business,' he snapped. I laughed at him and went out to church.

At the end of the worship period the pastor asked the visitors to stand. 'Let's all stand as we sing praises to God,' invited the pastor. At that point we turned round and saw my father standing there, head and shoulders above the rest. He was swaying, obviously more drunk than when I had left him at home.

'Look, Janaina, Father is here!' I said, and with that she ran and stood beside him.

As was his custom, the pastor preached a clear gospel message. 'Jesus said, "Come to Me, all you who are weary and burdened and I will give you rest" (Matt. 11:28). Jesus can lift your burdens; yes, the burden of every evil vice.'

'That's a lie,' shouted my drunken father from the back.

'Our God is mighty! He can deliver you from drink, from cigarettes and from lust.'

Loud laughter came from the rear.

'He can lift the burden of every problem.' The pastor continued his sermon in spite of the drunken shouting and laughing. At the end he gave an invitation to anyone who needed help to come forward. Father swaggered to the front with Janaina trailing him.

'I'm going to see if He can deliver me from alcohol and cigarettes,' he mocked loudly. He knelt at the altar and the pastor, in all sincerity, prayed for him. Suddenly the tipsy drunk stood erect, sober, quiet and respectful. The change was dramatic. I could not believe what I had just seen and heard.

At home I challenged him, 'Did you go forward in church to show off your new clothes?'

'Well, my first reason was to disturb the meeting,' he confessed. 'But when I knelt, something changed inside me. I can't understand or explain it, but I have changed. I'm new.'

His body still craved drink and cigarettes since he had smoked from the age of seven and was now smoking three packs every day. But by God's miracle, he never drank again and a few days later he gave up smoking. Though it was torture for him and he suffered physically, he still would not yield to temptation.

What a total change we witnessed! He eagerly attended meetings most days of the week. He took the bus when he could afford it, otherwise he walked. He used to urge me to read the Bible to him and he drank in every word. Everything changed. He no longer drank to cheer himself up. There were no more drunken jokes, frivolity or seeking the centre of attention. He now found his joy in Jesus Christ. The critical, lustful eyes became soft and loving, and instead of cursing he told others about Jesus and His power to transform lives.

Our transformed father recognised that we needed a new house. He had helped neighbours put up theirs as he was still muscular and strong although he was fifty-seven years old. He located a spot on another hillside and laid his claim. Up innumerable, treacherous steps he carried hundred-pound bags of sand, cement and bricks. My cousin Dico helped him for about two weeks, but he was bad news. He was involved with drugs, and stealing was his way of life. After his conversion, Father took him into our home and talked with him by the hour, pointing him to Jesus.

'God can change people. He can change you, too, Dico,' he told him.

'That's okay for you, Uncle, but religion isn't for me. I'm too young. It's time for you, not for me.' Although he seemed to respond positively at times and visited church once, he made no clear profession of salvation. One day he stole a toy from Janaina and disappeared. Two weeks later we went to his house to investigate. 'The Police caught him' was all that we were told and is all that we know to this day.

Jesus Christ forgave my father's sins and made a new man of him but in his body he carried the results of years of misuse. He was found to have cancer and six months after his conversion he discovered that he was dying. 'If it is His will,' he said, 'God can heal me. The Lord can do what He wants with my life.' There was no anger, just peace.

In March 1980, my father entered into the presence of his Saviour.

Spreading the light

Bible college

During my student years God put into my heart the desire to serve Him and I always assumed it would be in my own city, Rio de Janeiro. Before finishing university I wrote to three Bible Schools. I prayed to the Lord and said that I would apply to the first one that answered my inquiry. Betel Bible Institute answered first, sending me application forms. I had met the director, Dona Lidia, when she and a deputation team had presented a drama about revival.

I went to my pastor to ask him to write a recommendation for me to go to Betel. 'No,' he told me. 'You don't need to go to Bible School. I didn't, and God is using me.'

'Please. I need to know more about God and I want to study the Bible intensively.' Reluctantly, he wrote a brief letter and I was accepted to study at Betel.

What severe culture shock I encountered on moving from the big city of Rio de Janeiro, well south of the equator, to the small city of Joao Pessoa, almost on the equator in the northeast of Brazil! From the informal clothing of Rio de Janeiro to the prescribed uniform of the college: white blouses with sleeves to the elbow in school, or long sleeves when we went out, black skirt below the knees and black pumps! From living with my mother and Janaina to a first year dormitory room with twenty-six bunk beds! (The second and third year dorms were better with fewer beds.) I went from having the freedom to do my own thing to the rules and regulations of the college, including being told not to cut my hair! (I did, anyway, when it got long and bushy.)

In time I adjusted and came to appreciate the teaching and spirituality of Betel. I did the four-year seminary level course in three years (1982-1984) because my university degree was taken into consideration. Along with the class work, we went out in groups to do evangelism, church planting, and Christian education work.

Realisation of rape

At Bible School I had to see the doctor because I had some problems with my periods. I had a lot of pain and colic and every month I had to take strong pain-killers. The doctor asked me if I was a virgin. I said that I was, but when she finished examining me she was angry. She said I had lied to her.

The moment the doctor asked me why I had lied to her, I felt pain inside. I also felt very uncomfortable about that situation. In that moment many things came out: shame, despair, hate, sadness. I felt I was the worst person in the world. But I could not express it all to her, in spite of my 24 years. I was choked, and the only thing I could do was stare at her. No word came out from my mouth. She asked me if I wanted to speak about the situation, but all the kindness she had shown me at the beginning was gone. I was desperate to get out of that place.

I went back to the Bible School and all the remembrance of my childhood came out. It was a shock when I first understood what my father had done to me. Many people think autistic people don't have any feelings or perceptions. They live in a different world from others, certainly, one that would seem very strange to anyone else. But they do have feelings. They keep it all inside, or sometimes their reaction is to shout and scream about a situation that is bothering them. They cannot talk normally about it.

I had not understood till then how serious my father's actions had been and exactly what he had done to me. For the first time in my life I could understand the reasons for my hate and why I had avoided him for so long. I kept all these feelings inside myself and didn't say anything about them to anyone. But I did need healing, and started to pray about these feelings.

Called to Africa

It was 1984. This was my last year in Betel Bible Institute and graduation was near. My classmates talked about God calling them to specific places, but my future seemed to be uncertain which made me very anxious. The prayer room became my refuge. As I cried to the Lord for an answer, He led me to pray for Africa and its people. 'Lord Jesus,' I asked, 'are You calling me to Africa? Me?'

God moved in me in a way I had never felt before. 'Don't be afraid,' He said gently. 'I will be with you. I am your Father, your God and your strength. Be confident and rest in me.' I lacked confidence in people, in God and in myself. I had to learn it and build it up day by day. As I prayed for war-torn Mozambique, God supplied information and contacts. I would go there, I decided, war or no war.

At Betel we often had Mission Days when we focused on the needs of different continents. On one of these days I represented Africa, carrying the flag of Guinea-Bissau and for the first time I studied about this West African country. I began to wonder if God was calling me to Guinea-Bissau and not to Mozambique.

Bob Harvey, the WEC director in Brazil, gave us some lectures at Betel about cross-cultural missions. With his encouragement to look to Mozambique, I joined WEC early in 1985. For eight months I lived, worked and shared with missionaries and candidates as I studied English and did the candidate course. I collected prayer letters, photos and other information to include in the required project about Mozambique. I knew that for over a year devastating civil war had been raging there, people like moving skeletons were shown on television. But I believed, and still do, that the safest place on earth is in the centre of God's will, so I remained determined to go to Mozambique.

My plans frustrated

I returned to Rio de Janeiro to prepare for Africa, but when I told my pastor he just laughed in my face. 'I believe you can do a good work here. But Africa? You said Africa? Do you know where Africa is?' He laughed and laughed.

I had opportunities to preach, to talk about missions and give my testimony in many churches, but in my own church I was only allowed to give a short testimony two or three times. The people there never heard my whole testimony and so never knew about my life. They didn't know that I had been autistic, didn't know that my father had raped me, and didn't hear how God had worked in me to prepare me to become a missionary. (Even when I went home on furlough I never had the opportunity to share about my work in Africa.)

Repeatedly I went to the church in the hope of talking to my pastor. I wanted to talk to him about support or other ways in which I hoped the church would stand behind me. I told the church secretary I needed to talk with him. But the door was always shut. Once, while I was waiting to see the pastor, a well-dressed couple came to see him. He opened the door, greeted them cordially and invited them into his office. When he saw them to the door, I was still waiting. I had been waiting five hours.

Disappointed and frustrated, I turned to God. He had called me and He knows me. I recalled Job's reply to God; 'I know that you can do all things. No plan of yours can be thwarted' (Job 42:2). The next month I tried again to ask for the church's support but I was told that the church had no money to support anyone in Africa. They could only support me in prayer.

It was a blessing to have a WEC missionary, Miss Jani Vroegop, spend two days with us. She slept in our house, ate our food and saw all our difficulties. She met Bija and talked to her about Jesus. She heard the shooting from the bandits, but didn't comment on the situation. She talked to my pastor and after that the church began to give me a few small gifts. Back at the mission base she gave her report and some of the missionaries started to pray for a decent house in a better location for my family.

I was invited to many churches from various denominations to give my testimony. I didn't ask for money, and few of them gave me so much as my bus fare.

Pastor Marcos, founding pastor of a large church and president of his denomination, was an impressive man. Every year he bought the latest model of car. He seemed to have plenty of money. After visiting his church a few times, my mother talked with him. 'My daughter is going to Africa as a missionary. Would you be able to help her?'

'It would be a privilege. What does she need?'

'Well, she needs a suitcase, transportation to England and then to Africa and monthly support.'

'Bring her to church next Sunday morning. We're having a missionary conference. We'll be delighted to help her.' My mother came home happy with the news.

'Do you really think he will help me?' I asked repeatedly. 'If I go there and he doesn't give me any money, it will be just one more frustration.' But we went and found the church full.

After the music, he gave a twenty-minute Bible message.

Then for forty minutes he preached on money, after which they collected two big baskets of money. 'Dump this in my office,' he directed his assistant. 'And bring out another basket.' He then said to me, 'Come Margarida, I've told everybody that I'm going to help you.' He had me stand up at the front holding the large wicker basket with a metal bottom. Addressing the congregation, he began: 'Here is someone who is going to Africa. Africa needs people like her. They are poor. We are going to help her. Let's take up another offering.

He continued talking about me, telling them to give more money. They gave coins, the noise of which reminded me of begging. He kept urging them to give more. I was humiliated. The congregation was large, but the people were poor. They didn't have any more money. He had already taken all they could give.

After the service, he took me to his office and counted all those coins. 'Here is your help.' He smiled as he placed them into my hand. It was enough for the return bus fare for my mother and me.

'Bring our 'Missionary Suitcase', Miguel,' he called to his helper. 'This suitcase has been to Washington D.C., to Paraguay, to many places in Brazil.' On and on he went telling me the history of the 'Missionary Suitcase'. The dilapidated relic had a worn electric cable for a handle, it had holes, and it was torn and patched. My heart sank. How could I go to Europe with this suitcase? How could I go anywhere with it? I took the money and the suitcase. 'Thank you very much,' I said. 'It's a great help.'

Outside the church, my mother and I started to cry. I said to God, 'I want to go to the field, but this is no help. However, if this is what I am supposed to have, I thank you.' But I was very sad.

Unconventional help

In Copacabana, near the centre of the city, there was a well-known hairdresser, Joao Pedro, who specialised in varieties of plaiting. His early customers were all black, like himself. In 1979 Bija went to his ritzy place and asked for work. She was allowed to do the simple things: shampoo, roll hair, apply creams and give massages. The professionals did the cutting and special styles. After a year, she went to a beauty school where she became fully qualified to do everything in the trade.

In 1982, during vacation time from Bible School, I visited her at work. She told her boss that I plaited hair better than she did and that it was I who had taught her to plait. He asked me to demonstrate on an employee with long heavy hair. He was impressed with the speed, accuracy and beauty of my work and hired me on the spot. From that time on, whenever I was home in Rio de Janeiro, he always gave me work and said that I was the second best plaiter in the city.

For six months I worked diligently at hairdressing in order to save money. I told Joao Pedro that I was preparing to go to Africa via England.

'Do you have a big suitcase, Margarida?' he asked me one day.

'Nothing suitable,' I said, telling him about my relic.

His friend, Loretta, travelled regularly to Europe and had many suitcases. When he told her about me she decided to give me one, so I went to see her. 'Which one of these would you like?' she asked as she showed me a Brazilian, a French and two German suitcases. I thought about my few belongings and selected the smallest, simplest one. It was obviously the least expensive.

'No,' she said. 'I want to give you a better one. Which one do you want?'

'It's better that you choose for me because I don't know which one you want to give,' I replied. She selected the large German Executive Doce. (I used it until 1990 when it was stolen.) Before I could wonder how I would ever fill it up, she started pulling things out of cupboards and off shelves: sheets, blankets, bath towels, tea towels, underclothes, many of the things store-wrapped. She almost filled it even though she hardly knew me.

By plaiting hair I managed to save enough money for my flight to England. One day Joao Pedro asked me, 'Do you have any spending money, Margarida?'

'No.' I replied. Graciously he gave me $100.

During my first years in Africa two elderly ladies from the church sent small amounts. But it was my drug addict sister who was my main supporter.

Freedom

My sister Bija

Far from home, my thoughts often turned to Bija. When she was seventeen she had met Valter, aged fifteen. It was love at first sight. Together they danced. Together they took drugs. Together they had a child. Sadly, the little girl died after only a few days. One day Valter didn't show up and after that she didn't see him for years. He was out of her life.

For a year and half, in her early twenties, she lived as a Christian and gave up drugs. Then she fell in love with Roberto, a psychopathic drug addict, and married him. He was a beggar, eating food from rubbish bins. After five years he left her. She continued to live with us or with Roberto in a little home-made brick shack next to ours.

At church, someone accused her having a relationship with the assistant pastor. She denied it and was greatly offended. She stopped going to church. We urged her to try another one, but she didn't fit in there either. She tried the Baptist Church, then a Pentecostal Church and several others but still didn't find her place. Bit by bit she returned to her bad habits – first cigarettes, then marijuana, then back to cocaine, alcohol, and finally prostitution.

Unexpectedly, she received a letter from Valter. He was considered a dangerous criminal and had been in prison for many years. For two years she visited him, always taking him drugs. Visiting him in prison was equivalent to declaring that he was her man. A friend of hers told the police that Bija's bag had a false bottom and so she was searched, arrested and detained for five months. At the time I was in Africa and unaware of her imprisonment, but our dear mother visited her every week.

When an evangelist visited her, she told him to leave her alone. 'God isn't interested in me,' she declared. 'He's through with me. I'm at the end of my tether, walking through a deep, dark tunnel without end.'

The evangelist visited the prison frequently, each time stopping at her cell to assure her of God's love for her. He may not have known that she had a praying mother and sister, but God put it on his heart to be faithful in ministering to her.

The day came when her hardened shell broke and she yielded her life to Jesus. She was a new creature in Christ. Her prison behaviour and attitudes changed and tobacco addiction no longer had a grip on her. She shared with other prisoners about the power of Jesus Christ. Miraculously, Bija was not condemned and after five months was set free.

Then she found out that Valter had escaped from prison. They lived together for seven months in the two-roomed shack facing our mother's. Valter expected Bija to continue helping him with his drug trade, while she had high hopes that she could lead him to the Lord. At the same time, her hopes were mingled with the fear that he could murder her if she resisted him. He was furious that she had become a Christian and took it out on her with beatings and cigarette burns. He ordered her to leave her religion and work with him. Her only respite was working as a hairdresser.

She wrote to me, not mentioning either her time in jail or her conversion but only that she had changed, that she was with Valter and hoped that God could change him too. She filled her letter with scripture. I knew she was a new person.

She started to go to the Maranatha Church. It suited her and she loved to go there. Meanwhile, Valter kept pushing her to return to using and dealing with drugs. He searched for the money she earned as a hairdresser but she always left it with our mother. He hit Bija, beat her and burnt her with cigarettes but she steadfastly refused to have any part in his drug trade. God was at work in her.

One day she told our mother, 'God gave me a dream last night. He told me that I'm going to him soon.'

'No, my daughter. you're too young. You're not going to die.'

'Yes, Mother, I am. I saw not one, but two coffins. One was white, covered with beautiful flowers and the other was black.'

She began immediately to pay all her bills and debts. She wanted to enter her Saviour's presence debt free!

One Sunday morning at daybreak, Valter placed a necklace with a demonic charm on it in my mother's hand saying, 'Take this, Dona Zarita. I'm with the devil. I'm about to kill.' Although he might swear at her and give idle threats, he always treated her with respect.

All the previous night he had been beating Bija, burning her with cigarettes, swearing at her and destroying things she had bought. 'If she goes to the church,' he continued, 'I will kill her. I'm so angry that she goes there. She has to stop going to church and stop being a Christian. Give me that money she gave to you.'

'I will not give it to you. She gave it to me to pay the bills. The bills have to be paid.'

'I'm going for a gun.'

Committing her daughter to the Lord, my mother left to go prison visiting as she faithfully did every Sunday.

At 9.00 a.m. Valter returned and saw that Bija was ready for church. 'You are not going to church, woman!' he yelled.

'Oh, yes I am! If I'm alive, I'm going to church!' Bija rushed past him and ran around the corner of my mother's house, hurrying down the narrow passage between the buildings.

'If you do, I'm going to kill you,' he shouted, pulling out his gun.

'Kill. I'm going. My friend Claudia is waiting for me.'

He shot her three times. She fell in the open sewer ditch in the middle of the path. As Valter ran away, screaming neighbours, who loved Bija, carried her to the road, located a car and accompanied her the short distance to the hospital.

She was admitted to hospital at 11.00 a.m. and at 12:30 p.m. she spoke her last words: 'Jesus, I knew I was going to die because You told me. But I didn't want it to be this way.'

At the same time, Valter was being brought into the same hospital after an encounter with a policeman which had ended his life. They died at the same time.

The druggies gave my mother money for the funeral and she bought a beautiful white pine coffin for Bija, which friends covered with flowers. She bought a dark cardboard coffin for Valter.

Then I heard a voice from heaven say, 'Write: Blessed are the dead who die in the Lord from now on.' 'Yes,' says the Spirit, 'they will rest from their labour, for their deeds will follow them'. (Rev. 14:13)

'And I saw an angel coming down out of heaven... I saw thrones on which were seated those who had been given authority to judge. And I saw the souls of those who had been beheaded because of their testimony for Jesus and because of the word of God. They had not worshipped the beast or his image and had not received his mark upon their foreheads or their hands. They came to life and reigned with Christ a thousand years... This is the first resurrection. Blessed and holy are those who have part in the first resurrection. The second death has no power over them, but they will be priests of God and of Christ and will reign with Him for a thousand years.' (Rev. 20: 1, 4-6)

When a friend of Bija's wrote to me to tell me about her death, I cried, 'Oh, God! Why did You allow her to see that man again after all those years? Why did You allow him to kill her? I want to see my mother, to see how she is.'

My mother didn't have a phone, and neither did any of the neighbours. So I phoned my mother's church in Rio de Janeiro. 'Did you know my sister was killed?' I asked. 'Have you visited my mother? Has anyone from the church visited her?'

'Oh, your mother's fine. She's alive,' replied the church secretary.

'Did the pastor conduct the funeral?'

'No. Bija hadn't been going to our church.'

'I really need to go home to see my mother, to be with her. Could the church loan me the money to go home?'

'I'll see what the pastor says,' was her reply. After another phone call and another plea for help, the reply came: 'No. The pastor told me that the church doesn't have the money for this. You are wasting your money phoning here. We don't have any money to give you. Please don't phone here again.' She hung up.

I started crying, 'God, I don't have the money but I want to go home.'

I didn't tell many people about what had happened, only my three closest fellow-missionaries. One of them told my church in Guinea-Bissau, and a Guinean medical doctor who had studied in Brazil came to my house asking if I would be going home to see my mother. I told him I couldn't, but didn't tell him why. One of my friends told him that it was because I didn't have the money. He decided to encourage the church to raise the money for me. I needed $2000. How could the Africans, who have so little money, raise that amount? I saw many of them selling their chickens and valuable things to raise the money. Within ten days I had the money and was ready to go. Most of it had come from the Africans and some from my fellow-missionaries, Rosa and Isa. I was able to visit my mother for several weeks.

Out of the slums

I had graduated from university, been to Bible School, been accepted by WEC International, studied linguistics in England, spent three and a half years in Guinea-Bissau and was now back home on furlough, living in the slums. Dad and Bija had died but my mother was still living in the slum on the steep mountainside. We were still plagued by poverty and violence. Drug-related shootings were common.

Walking home from the bus one Sunday evening after church, we suddenly saw a crowd of drug dealers on the path ahead of us. They had surrounded five terrified individuals and were engaged in a heated argument. I was carrying Janaina's darling, chubby eight-month-old daughter, Pamela, while my mother was holding on to Janaina. To the left of our narrow dirt path was a barbed wire fence guarding a six-foot drop, to the right was the wall of a building. So to reach our shack we had to pass through the midst of them. We knew the leader; Rat was his nickname.

'Get going,' he barked at us. 'Run. We have work to do. Get out of here! Run! Run!'

Janaina pulled my mother along and I followed, struggling to carry Pamela who weighed more than twenty-two pounds. We had to climb many steps up the hill to our house. We were no more than thirty metres from the drug dealers when they started shooting the five they had surrounded. Fearful, we raced to our house. An eerie silence descended.

At 6:45 next morning I set out for work at the hairdresser's. I rounded the corner of our home and saw lying there, in the narrow path between the buildings, a disembodied head. Staring at it, I recognised it as belonging to one of those five. Terrified, I looked from side to side. An arm to the right! A bare leg to the left! Other body parts! All covered with dry blood! My heart pounded within me. Shaking with fright, I ran back to the house. I burst into the house, waking Janaina. I called to my mother: 'Those drug dealers shot and killed those five and cut them all up. They threw parts of their bodies everywhere.'

After this my mind was made up. I could not return to Africa and leave my mother, Janaina and Pamela living in this violent territory. As was my custom, I turned to my Heavenly Friend, 'God,' I said, 'I will not stay in this place any more. The five murders last night were too much. I've had enough.' After the police cleared away the bodies, I ventured out to my job.

Later that week I visited Rosane, a good friend from a well-to-do family. I told her that I needed to move my mother because it was too violent where we lived. We spent a considerable time discussing the situation. Then she picked up a book to show me. 'This is a tremendous book,' she said. 'Have you ever heard of it? It's about breaking hereditary curses. I've just finished reading it. Here, take it and read it.'

As I read the book over the next couple of days, I was able to link many things from my past and from my family with what the author was saying. Things I had never been able to understand were clarified. I began to realise that the author was writing about situations like mine. Was an hereditary curse the key to my problems? I thought back on my life. We had never had anything. Until I was ten we had lived in just one room. I had never had a bed but slept on an old sofa or on the floor. I had never had a room to myself. We never bought anything. We had just what other people gave us: old things and broken things. And here we were now, living in an unfurnished house that my father had started building after he retired. The walls were unplastered, there were no inside doors. It had a ceiling but no roof and had just the minimum of electrical wiring. Even though we had three small bedrooms, two were unusable because the floors were rotten. Added to this, the location was so dangerous! We heard shootings and gang wars all the time and bullets often flew through the house.

In Africa other Brazilian missionaries had things but I didn't. I had to borrow from everybody. I didn't have any money and was always in need.

'I'm fed up,' I told my mother. 'For twelve years, I've worked for the Lord. We've given our tithes and offerings and yet we still don't have anything.' Then I told her about the book. 'Tell me, did anything ever happen in our family to hold us in this poverty trap?'

'Before your grandfather died we had things,' she told me. 'But we lost everything. He told me once that he had made a pact with the devil for prosperity, but all we ever got was poverty.'

My mother, Janaina and I sat on the bed and talked about the problems in our family. We agreed that we were experiencing a curse of poverty and had to break it. We had been living in misery but knew we couldn't keep on living this way. My mother slipped to her knees and I prayed for the three of us. 'We break this curse of poverty, misery, drugs, alcohol, prostitution and vice in the name of Jesus.' We prayed together. We saw nothing and felt nothing, but God began to work.

Two months earlier I had attended a missionary conference in Sao Paulo where I was asked to tell my story. I described how no churches had helped me but God had used my drug addict/beautician sister to send me support. He had used a spiritist hair salon manager to give me work with good pay. He used a sophisticated Godless lady to give me an elegant suitcase full of things that I needed. After my testimony the officiating pastor called the other pastors to the front to repent for not having helped me, and he asked me to pray for them.

A week after breaking the curse, miracles began to happen. One of those pastors invited me to his Congregational church on the other side of Rio de Janeiro to speak about my life.

'When will you be returning to Africa?' he asked me.

'First I'm going to buy a house' I replied. 'Then I'll return to Africa.'

Afterwards, while we were eating, a couple spoke to me: 'We live in a cul-de-sac near here. It's a good place and a calm area. One of the twenty-two houses is up for sale. There is everything locally that your mother would need.'

'How much is it?' I asked.

'Fifteen thousand dollars.'

We went to see it. It had a bedroom big enough for two single beds, a wardrobe and dresser; a small living room; a tiny bathroom and a compact kitchen. Outside were laundry facilities.

As soon as I could I phoned the owner. Altogether, with additional costs, I needed $17,000. The owner told me that he had four other prospective buyers but would give me a week to find the money, otherwise he would sell it to someone else. I had already received a gift of $12,000 for the house, so I prayed and asked God to provide the remaining $5,000 that week. Within a few days another large gift arrived. Money came in many ways and I was able to buy the house. We took the refrigerator and TV from our old house but I was able to buy everything else new.

'The Lord is almighty and has taken us from the slums!' exclaimed my mother.

For decades she has risen early to read the Bible and pray. Every morning, at 6 o'clock, she walks two blocks to her church for an hour of prayer with six to ten others. She has continued visiting three prisons where, even at the age of eighty-four, she preaches the Word of God with power. She is dearly loved in her church and neighbourhood as well as in her family. Her sorrow has turned to joy and she rejoices in the faithfulness of God.

Back in 1986, when I was in England, Jani, a missionary friend, had written to her sister in Holland about me. Her sister then invited me to visit her and during that delightful vacation I visited several churches. Later, when Jani was on furlough, she also shared with them about my situation. At the very time the curse was broken my Dutch friends sent me money.

God provided a regular supporter for the first time. My situation changed both in Brazil and in Africa. My conditions got so much better and improved month by month, year by year. I pray for things and God provides them. I've been able to travel home from Africa each year to check on my mother. I've not been rich, but God has supplied my needs.

New church

In January 1993, while I was in Sao Paulo, I phoned my friend, Elizeu. He had talked with his pastor about me and encouraged me to go and see him. I attended a Friday service in the parsonage. There the pastor asked me to give my testimony and after listening to me for two hours he said: 'We are going to help you. If you want us to fully support you we would like you to join our church.' When they received me, my new pastor said, 'I'm receiving another daughter.'

And that is what it felt like to me. It was the beginning of a new time for me. I thank God for the way he has helped me through this new church. Even though it is not in my hometown, I love it. They have supported me faithfully. They write to me and have helped me in many ways.

Back in Rio, when I told the secretary of my old church why I was leaving, I asked if I could talk briefly with the pastor to explain to him why I wanted to change membership. He refused to see me. Later that same year, while I was in England, I wrote to him although I would have preferred to have talked with him personally. After all, for nineteen years my mother had attended his church. He had baptised me and had shown me God's will concerning my healing. It was under his ministry that my father had come to Jesus. I thanked him for the money he had given me the last time I was at his church. It had supplemented money from other churches to pay for a gas freezer and solar lamp. I explained that having the freezer I could purchase fish, beef and other food items and keep them for up to a year and so didn't have to do the three-hour trip to Bissau so often. I unburdened my heart, and reminded him of the many ways he had discouraged me. I told him that it was because of these things that I had decided to find another church where I could be supported both financially and spiritually.

I received no reply. The next time I went to Brazil I asked him if he had received my letter.

'Yes, I received it,' was all he said.

* * *

I praise God for leading my mother to a church near our new home where she is loved and enjoys good prayer fellowship. God helped her face up to the financial crisis in Brazil when everything became too expensive to buy. I was concerned about her and wrote asking how she was getting on. She sent a letter in reply saying that although Janaina had been dismissed from her job, within two weeks she had found a better paid one.

Mauricio, a pastor from a Baptist church in Rio, has helped my mother since 1991 with money and gifts. This has been the best time of her life since I left Brazil. What a wonderful God we have who can work miracles in our personal lives. He cares for us. Another Baptist church gives her help monthly and the Congregational church nearby gives her many kinds of food.

Deliverance from curses

Early in 1994, at the Bible School in N'tchumbe, Guinea-Bissau, I received a sermon on cassette from a Brazilian pastor about breaking curses, including ancestral curses. I recognised that I had always been easily hurt. My parents and grandparents had been deceived by the devil and had been bound by such things as drug addiction, sexual promiscuity and abuse, illness and spiritism. God had broken the curse of poverty two years before and now for three hours God led me to break these other curses. I wrote in my Bible, 'Today I have broken all the curses that have

bound me in the past.' I didn't experience freedom immediately, but day by day I saw changes especially regarding how easily I could be hurt or become bitter.

Over the past years I have learnt many things. We are in the
midst of battles that we can't escape. That's why we must pray
all the time without stopping. If we stop praying we become
weak and lose the battle. I have been set free from the traumas,
the bitterness and the sadness of heart that always led me to be
unsociable. I have started doing things I had never been able to
do before. I can now carry on long conversations, laugh and be
sociable. I've always found it difficult to make friends, but the
Lord has given me security and confidence so that I no longer
feel threatened and now have been able to make several close
friends. When I think of this song it reminds me of how the Lord
has worked in me:

> Oh Lord, Your tenderness melting all my bitterness,
> Oh Lord, I receive Your love.
> Oh Lord, Your loveliness changing all my ugliness,
> Oh Lord, I receive Your love.

Knowing that the Lord is able to do all things, I can now face
the unknown, the impossible and the unreachable. I can trust in
His unfailing love and His compassion and keep pressing forward.

> For our struggle is not against flesh and blood, but against the
> rulers, against the authorities, against the powers of this dark
> world and against the spiritual forces of evil in the heavenly
> realms. Therefore put on the full armour of God, so that when
> the evil day comes, you may be able to stand your ground,
> and after you have done everything, to stand. (Eph. 6:12,13)

WEC missionary

Challenges abroad

To work in harmony with an international mission like WEC I
needed to learn English, the international language of the mission. I was about to buy my ticket to London to start language
study when word came through that all missionaries had been
withdrawn from Mozambique because of the war and political

situation. I thought about it for a week. I recalled holding Guinea-Bissau's flag in that pageant when we were challenged with, 'Who will go?' and we had all replied in unison 'Here am I, send me.' I knew that the Guinea-Bissau Bible Institute was short-staffed and that I could help them and I felt, perhaps, that this was where God was leading me. But first, it was off to England for ten months' language study.

It was a cold, foggy day when I arrived in London. Wilma, my Brazilian friend, came to the airport to collect me, so I didn't have any difficulties. But when I arrived at the UK WEC headquarters, a large house called Bulstrode, my struggles began. My time in England was a big challenge. I shared a bedroom with five other girls who came from Germany, Holland, Switzerland, Finland and Brazil. At that time I still had difficulties expressing myself and was very shy. People had to make the first contact with me and then I could become a good friend. English people are reserved and compared to Brazilians they appear to be cold.

When Wilma went to Portugal I was alone most of the time. But the Lord gave me some angels to help me: Mike and Pauline Brogden, Bill Elcock, Mamie Freitag and Jill Johnstone. At Christmas Jill invited Wilma and me to her house to have supper. When I arrived she gave me a big hug but I didn't respond as she expected me to. I didn't respond like a Brazilian and she sensed that I was uncomfortable with it. I explained that I didn't like hugs and kisses and told her a bit about my past. By then Jill, Pauline and Wilma were the ones that I could go to and ask for help. I found in them love and kindness. Even after so many years since my healing, I was still learning how to relate to people. I helped Pauline in the kitchen and she helped me a lot with my English studies, took me shopping and sometimes took me to her church though usually I went to Gold Hill Baptist Church where I grew to love the people, the worship and the ministry. Bill helped me a lot with my understanding of the English language and corrected me with kindness. I spent a lot of time in front of the TV so my understanding of the English language progressed much faster than my ability to speak.

After being in England for about four months I sat the Cambridge First Certificate in English. I passed with a good grade and so I was ready to do a linguistics course run by Wycliffe Bible Translators. This was a time when more of the barriers in my life were broken down. We were in class most of the time but we took a break every afternoon to play volleyball. The other students were young and cheerful, like some Brazilians. There the Lord did more miracles in my life. I didn't have much money, nowhere near enough to pay for the course. The director of Wycliffe asked me if I had the faith to start the course believing that God would provide the money for it. I said that I did, and to my surprise two weeks before the course finished the Lord sent twice the amount of money that I needed. The Lord is so faithful to me. The money helped me to buy many things that I needed for Guinea-Bissau.

When I went back to Bulstrode, things were different. The people hadn't changed, but I had. I started to open up more and my opinion changed regarding English people's reserve. I was touched by their farewell for me. It was the first one that I'd had. Even now they still remember me and I thank God for them.

After language study I needed to obtain a visa for Guinea-Bissau. I could get one in Portugal which meant I did not have to travel all the way back to Brazil. After a few days in Portugal and with my visa in hand, I boarded a plane for Guinea-Bissau. It was September 1987. On the plane I became terrified by the loud, black Africans with all their excess luggage and electronic equipment. I felt hemmed in. The person seated next to me was drinking heavily and kept asking me personal questions in Creole, a language of Guinea-Bissau. I tried to get out of the conversation by feigning sleep.

When we landed at one o'clock in the morning, the airport was dark. Everything was black; the people, the air and the airport. Candles provided the only light. I collected my luggage and passed through immigration. Everybody around me was speaking a foreign language. There was no one there to meet me and the place quickly emptied. There were no taxis. I felt very vulnerable and frightened waiting there alone. I asked God to send someone to help me. I sat on my luggage, holding onto everything I had.

Four hours after my plane had landed, a man approached and asked me if I was Margarida. I looked up to see a bushy-bearded white man. He reminded me of my father, being tall with a long face and nose. (My father's grandfather had come from Holland.) Hans Frinsel, a Dutch missionary, had come to take me to the mission.

Adjustment to the high humidity, multitudinous mosquitoes and different foods came hard. Headaches and intestinal problems were my lot. The mission was in disarray. Leadership was entrusted to a committee. No one was assigned to guide my orientation. I had to learn everything myself and could do much as I pleased, which suited me. Areta McBride, who had been there for over thirty years, helped me a lot. She explained the culture and showed me the country.

A first-year missionary from Hong Kong and a Guinean lady took me to the market and other places. I began to learn the ways of the people and the Creole language. The markets were meagre: stinking dried fish, charcoal, and okra but no other vegetables or fruit. Rice, full of bugs and smelling awful, was available in the big government store. Because Guinea-Bissau had suffered a devastating drought, there was a food shortage in the country. Some of our missionaries travelled occasionally to Senegal where their children studied and would return with food.

A month after I arrived, cholera struck the area. I had stomach problems that looked like cholera but, praise God, it wasn't. People were dying on every side. They were unable to care for themselves. Ignorant of the cause of the contamination, the survivors took the dead into their homes, thus exposing all the family to the disease. In one family I knew, only an infant girl survived. I was appalled. I had never seen so much death.

Bible School teaching

The Bible School in Bissau, the capital city, was short of teachers, so three months after my arrival I started to teach five subjects (in the official language of Portuguese): Portuguese grammar and composition, homiletics, Ephesians, geography and New Testament studies.

The Central Church in Bissau had about 180 members but no pastor. For three-and-a-half years I was given the responsibility of this church. I helped with the women, children, discipleship and preaching. Two elderly Guinean men, who had studied in Bible School long before, also helped with the preaching. Being a young woman in Guinea-Bissau, my preaching was not always accepted, especially by Muslim men. Men, particularly the elderly, have the last word. I had to consult them on everything. I had to ask the Lord to calm me and teach me humility so that I could get things done. With twenty-seven tribes and twenty-two languages in the country, cultural adjustment is difficult even for them. We all thought differently. I had to learn to accept others and not to humiliate them, to submit, to consult and to respect the opinions of others. To me they seemed ignorant but I learned 'Honour one another above yourselves' (Romans 12: 10b), and that 'unless a grain of wheat falls to the ground and dies, it remains only a single seed. But if it dies, it produces many seeds' (John 12: 24).

I also learned that God is faithful. The faithfulness of God was so real in my life, especially in the beginning when I didn't have much support. I went to church several times a week. When I didn't have enough money for the bus I had to walk for an hour-and-a-half, often in the hot sun. Sometimes I wanted to buy something from the local people to support their work, but I didn't have the money. But I saw God's faithfulness and always had enough money to pay my bills.

For five months that first year I received no money due to postal problems, but a fellow Brazilian missionary had money and helped me. One night as I lay on my bed, I asked God for some meat as I didn't have the money to buy any. First thing the next morning my friend came round with a leg of deer. He gave me a good portion of it and I cooked some for him. Sometimes when I didn't have any money to buy food, friends would bring some for me to prepare and cook for them. In this way I had some good meals.

During the summer vacation the teachers offered twenty-five short Bible courses which helped many of the believers who didn't have a good understanding of the Bible. They received teaching on the books of Moses and the life of the church.

Late in October we started our new Bible School year. Besides teaching four subjects I translated many textbooks and arranged and scheduled the students' preaching. When we finished the Bible School term in January the students went out for practical Christian experience for the next month while I prepared my subjects to teach when they returned. In June eight students graduated, a married man, four single men and three single ladies. They filled the need for pastors and workers for the next year in many needy areas.

That year the church in Guinea-Bissau celebrated its fiftieth anniversary. We sought to evangelise the whole nation. Our church was assigned to Bolama Island where the majority were young people, the Bijagos Islands (twenty islands without believers and four islands with believers) and Bafata, a city in the interior where 90% of the population is Muslim. Before setting out to evangelise, we studied the book of Joshua with the theme 'Forward'. We heard God speaking, not just to Joshua but to us also to go out and reach our land.

Without a pastor, the dedicated elders and enthusiastic youth leaders worked with me. They led groups to visit many parts of Guinea where there were few or no believers. In each place people became Christians. During that Year of Evangelism, I visited Uno, Orango and Bolama, all Bijagos islands.

Tough times

After my first home leave, I returned to Guinea-Bissau for another year. It was a year of challenges. I had many attacks of malaria. I broke my leg. I caught a severe abdominal infection. I lost a lot of weight and I found out that I had an ulcer.

That year I went to a youth camp on the island of Bolama, expecting to have some fun to relieve my depression. A lad and I were responsible for the kitchen. We had only one barrel of water for the kitchen, just enough for food and drink. It was fine for the first two days but my fun was short lived. A twenty-five-year-old camper wanted some of that precious water to wash the dishes. I objected, reminding him that it was needed for cooking. But he wouldn't listen.

'No, it's my water,' he objected. 'It's my country. I can do what I want with my water.' Becoming very angry, he started to take water, using it so wastefully that he used half the barrel.

'You are being wilfully disobedient,' I said. 'It's not a Christian way of behaving.'

Taking offence because I had spoken to him as to a naughty child, he yelled at me, grabbed me by the front of my shirt and slammed me repeatedly against the wall. Shocked, I took it silently, but others saw him, 'What are you doing?' they remonstrated. 'Are you crazy? She has her reasons. She is responsible and this water is for the kitchen.'

'She's a foreigner,' he replied. 'She has no right to say anything.'

I was very upset. Afterwards they took us to the pastor, who supported the camper, and said I was in the wrong. 'I don't want to come back here,' I decided. I was depressed and disappointed with everything.

It was also a year of break-ins. I had accepted the invitation to support my dear friend Marizete in her marriage to a British man in England. I would be her only compatriot and friend of long standing. When I went to the camp I had left my beautiful suitcase, packed with things for the wedding, in the field leader's house for safety. After the camp I found out that my suitcase had been stolen and everything in it – my treasured camera, money for the airfare, my new shoes and all my best clothes. I concluded from this that the Lord didn't want me to be in Guinea-Bissau. The field leader's wife, Amy Cuthbert, burst into tears when she found out because it had been stolen from her house. But I stood there with no emotion showing, temporarily reverting back to the characteristics of my youth.

I had just read a book called 'Winning by Losing'. In it the author taught that every time you lose something you will receive more. Jesus said, 'Whoever loses his life for me will find it' (Matt. 16: 25). The Lord showed me that He would make it up to me. But I needed to pay my airfare immediately and didn't know how I was going to get it. Elizeu, a fellow missionary from Brazil, loaned me money for the flight to England.

Recuperation abroad

I arrived at London airport gaunt, exhausted and bent over with pain because of a bleeding duodenal ulcer. I was met by a representative from the mission headquarters who drove his silent passenger to Bulstrode.

At the one meal I ate there, a friendly Indian visitor talked with me, asking about my work. Later that day Ann, a friend of Marizete, came and took me to her home. While with her I was able to see a doctor and begin treatment. She and her husband took good care of me and by the wedding day I was standing up straight and feeling very much better.

Much to my surprise I received a telephone call from my new Indian acquaintance. He called to tell me that he had deposited money for me in my account. Praise the Lord! It was twice the amount that I needed. The Bulstrode staff also gave me another gift.

Even after ten weeks of Ann's good care, I was still too weak to travel to Brazil where too much would have been expected of me. However, Wilma, my Brazilian friend in Portugal invited me to continue my recuperation at her home. After two months with her I was ready to return to Brazil.

I returned to Brazil for a year, 1991-1992, and I was glad to have my old job back doing hair for Joao Pedro.

Jungle Bible School

The Bible School closed temporarily when we left the cramped quarters in the capital city and began building a new campus in the jungle, in the area of N'tchumbe. The National Church President had asked the government for land and was offered a large tract that for generations had been 'sacred' to the evil spirits. The Guinean President never expected the church to accept it because it was a place feared by the local people as 'Satan's abode' and called 'the way of the serpent'. But the church gladly accepted this isolated place some 140 kilometres north of the capital city. It was beautiful, having a river for fishing, a jungle with wild boar, gazelle and deer, farm land so that students could work for their support, and plenty of room for expansion. The problems with the land were the snakes, and the witch doctor who refused to vacate. He put fetishes (objects of evil spirit worship) in our way and performed blood sacrifices against us. Some of the locals were afraid of this but we looked to God to break the power of Satan and bring salvation to these people.

We moved to the campus in August 1993 even though it still lacked the kitchen, bathrooms, running water and many other things. To me, N'tchumbe was a blessing from God. I had always lived in big cities like Rio de Janeiro but here I could enjoy the peace and quiet, listen to the birds singing and watch the wild animals. Here in the jungle, I really felt for the first time that I was in Africa. Lacking beef, we ate monkeys, wild boar and deer. We grew our own rice and vegetables. The first term we harvested 316 pumpkins. God has continued to bless us very much here. We don't have any support besides our crops. The students pay very little, insufficient to cover their food. The Guinean churches send support from time to time, which is appreciated, but it is still insufficient. We sell some of our produce in order to buy groceries.

At first I found life with only a few co-workers lonely, but I praise God for good friendship with the students and children. During that time I carried a heavy load teaching seven subjects, including Portuguese, Homiletics, Geography and Bible survey, each for one or two hours a week. I was also responsible for the catering for over forty people, planning, shopping and directing the cooks. This involved a monthly two-day trip to the city for supplies.

On Friday nights we had a prayer meeting, Saturday evenings we had a social time and on Sundays we had regular services. The students visited other churches once a month and it was my responsibility to organise these preaching visits.

The challenge of Islam

Islam, the dominant religion in eastern Guinea-Bissau where our Bible School is located, presents a formidable challenge. As I prepared lessons about Islam, it seemed that demons were attacking me with illness. A group of sixteen YWAM (Youth With A Mission) workers who were also reaching out to Muslims were similarly attacked. We travelled around local villages sharing the gospel with the people. Some villages received us, but only to discuss the merits of Islam. Even now we continue to visit them to present the gospel of Jesus Christ, but it seems that we are butting our heads against a high, thick wall that can neither be scaled nor penetrated. The spirit that controls Islam is strong, but our God is sovereign and ready to save. This is our motivation.

We faced stiff opposition in a village called Bidjin. Angrily the leaders gathered the people to pelt us with stones and chase us away. Courageously, the pastor began to preach under the anointing of the Holy Spirit. The power of the Lord was so strong that the ring-leader shut his mouth immediately. We stood in awe as we watched him listening to the Word. After the preaching he and another man said, 'You can come again. We have misunderstood your God. You have a very good religion. We want to hear more.' The next time we went, 70 people sat listening to the gospel. Afterwards the leader asked if we would go back again. The people in this village are totally open to the gospel.

In a region which a few years ago had no disciples of Christ with an Islamic background, there are now several. They need our prayer support as they are persecuted and abandoned by their families. The devil is never willing to allow anyone to go without a struggle. But the powerful hand of the Lord is with them and He can deliver them.

God said to Moses, 'I AM WHO I AM... But I know that the King of Egypt will not let you go, unless a mighty hand compels him. So I will stretch out my hand and strike the Egyptians with all my wonders that I will perform among them. After that, he will let you go.' (Ex.3: 14a, 19, 20)

God's deliverance

The Balanta village of Meru, just 28 kilometres from N'tchumbe, is under a curse because their ancestors made a pact with the devil in order to gain prosperity and to help their dying children. The devil gave them everything, cattle and healthy children, but then he removed the water from the village. In the dry season they have to walk eight to ten kilometres for water. Humanitarian aid organisations have attempted to dig wells there but they have dug down more than a hundred metres without striking water. The village wants to break this curse but they are afraid of the devil. They accept our preaching of the gospel, but only one old man has been converted. He said to us, 'I'm afraid of the spirits. But as you said that your God is so powerful I will believe what you say and will accept it even though I know that it will be very difficult.' He was right. After his conversion the persecution began. It was very hard for him as a former alcoholic especially when caju wine was being made in the village. A student sometimes bikes the 28 kilometres to teach him the Word. He stands alone, an outcast, but he has continued firm in the faith.

* * *

A poor wine maker experienced deliverance from the power of the devil through Christ. She scalded herself with hot caju wine and was in great pain and covered in scars when we met her in the government hospital. She told us she wanted to accept Christ but first she would have to go back to her village and make sacrifices to calm the evil spirits. We had a good talk with her and explained that Jesus is the All-Powerful One whom no one can defeat. She was so pleased to hear this and gave her life to Christ.

* * *

A group from our church visited an island in the Atlantic Ocean and found a village that had never heard the name of Jesus. We saw a woman comatose with fever. She may have had cerebral malaria. The elder who was with us offered to pray for her, telling the people that God could heal her. The local witch doctor mocked, 'For two weeks I have been praying for her, doing incantations and it hasn't worked. Do you think that your God can help her?'

'Yes, He can!' the elder replied. 'Let's pray for her.'

Although her husband, the village leader, was sceptical, he let us pray for her. We asked them to remove all their fetishes and then we prayed for fifteen minutes. Afterwards the woman got up and asked for food. She was completely healed.

'I want to know Jesus. Which one is Jesus?' her husband asked. He thought that one of us was Jesus! We explained who Jesus is and a few days later he became a Christian.

* * *

Luisa was possessed with demons. She tried to commit suicide three times and sometimes a demon came into her body and paralysed her. She knew it was the work of the devil. We learned that she was the mother of five small children and was married to an evil man with a high position. She had been brought up by an aunt who had prepared her to take her place as the village witch. Luisa had learned to preside over animal sacrifices, incantations and ceremonies. She had learned to make contact with demons in order to heal and tell fortunes.

In 1994, a lady from the Central Church in Bissau kept inviting her to church. Eventually she visited the church. When people were asked to go to the front for prayer she began to scream. She lost control of her face and other parts of her body. Her arms became paralysed. She was taken into another room where people continued to pray for her.

Pastor Jose Paulo and others from the church visited her in

her home, prayed for her and with her consent began casting out the demons. They stayed with her for days; although he was very tired, the pastor did not give up until all the demons had been cast out. Then Pastor Jose Paulo asked her if she wanted to be saved. She was ready.

Within a month her aunt died. In order to inherit both the demonic and material inheritances, Luisa was expected to wash the body, perform animal sacrifices and make a new alliance with the devil. The body couldn't be buried until all these things were accomplished. The family pressurised Luisa to comply but she refused to travel to the funeral. The devil tried to tempt her by reminding her of all the things she would lose if she didn't do the sacrifices. She was confused, but God also showed her what she would have if she held firm. Meanwhile the decaying body waited thirteen days until a strange voice came from the mouth of a child belonging to her family. It said that since Luisa would not fulfil her obligation she did not belong to their people any more and they could bury the body. From the mouth of the child the demon told Luisa that if she didn't do what they required, they would kill her.

Luisa forfeited her land, house, cattle and money. Her husband lost his business and went into debt. They became destitute. Some months later, in 1995, her husband accepted the Lord and became a real man of God and Luisa has remained a strong Christian in the church. God is our deliverer. When we trust in Him, He gives the victory.

God's protection

N'tchumbe is a jungle with sinister visitors. One dark, moonless night I stepped out of the house to turn off the water as the water drums were full. From the light of my solar lamp I saw, less than half a metre away from me, a shiny, black, poisonous snake. It was about three metres long and its jaw was open wide. I could not shout. I could not move. I was paralysed with fright and stood there trembling.

It started to spit poison at me and I cried out, 'Jesus! I'm afraid.' Then a frog appeared. The snake looked back and forth from the frog to me, spitting each time. Finally, it decided to swallow the frog. Relieved, I went back inside the house, carefully shutting the door behind me and called an African student to come and kill the snake. He came with a big stick but when he saw the snake he was afraid. He needed a gun to kill this one! That day I knew that God was by my side protecting me.

> But now, this is what the LORD says—
> He who created you, O Jacob,
> He who formed you, O Israel:
> 'Fear not, for I have redeemed you;
> I have called you by name; you are mine.' (Isa.43:1)

* * *

Rosa and I had been visiting an island off the coast of Guinea-Bissau and were returning in a large open canoe with a 35 horse-power motor. In the canoe were three cows, three or four pigs, chickens and about forty people, mostly women and children, all crammed in, unable to move. It normally took about four-and-a-half hours from the island to Bissau city. We departed at 4.00 am, at high tide, because the canoe goes faster with the help of the current. We should have docked before the sun got hot and been with friends for breakfast, but it didn't quite work out like that.

The captain and most of the men on board got drunk and the captain fell sound asleep. We were in the middle of the channel when a storm arose. The waves lifted the canoe and then slammed us down on the ocean, making us all sick. We were lost and didn't know what to do. Meanwhile the captain was still in a drunken sleep. Tense with fear I started to sing:

> Master, the tempest is raging,
> The billows are tossing high!
> The sky is o'er shadowed with blackness,
> No shelter or help is nigh;
> Carest Thou not that we perish?
> How canst Thou lie asleep;
> When each moment so madly is threat'ning
> A grave in the angry deep?

Rosa joined in singing with me. When we started singing the words of Jesus 'Peace be still!' the sea started to calm down. We started to pray.

When the captain awoke some hours later, there were no islands in sight. Realising we were off course, he turned the boat around. There was only one gallon of fuel left for the motor. It took us another five hours to get back on our route. We finally arrived in Bissau at 1.00 am. Our four-hour trip had taken twenty hours. We were sick, soaked and starving, but alive and safe.

> When you pass through the waters,
> I will be with you;
> And when you pass through the rivers,
> they will not sweep over you... (Isa 43:2a)

*   *   *

The risk of fires is very high in the dry season. Once we seemed to be surrounded by fire and it felt like hell. Perhaps that is a strong way of saying it but it was what it felt like at the time. Not having sufficient water to quench the fire, we had to take green branches and attempt to beat it out. It was a struggle that lasted for many hours. The students, staff, women and children worked together. All our fields were burnt; the orange, lemon and palm trees, potatoes and rice were all destroyed. Only a little manioc was left.

How did the fire start? It could have been in any number of ways. The local people use fire to clear the jungle of dry leaves and to force out the animals so that the hunters can spot them. The wine-makers make holes in the palm trees and collect wine in a pail. Before doing so they need to burn out the snakes. Some villages burn the rice fields to clear them ready for the next planting season. So every year fires are started and get out of control but every year God has saved us from them. Sometimes in the middle of the night we have had to go out to fight a fire but God is so faithful and He has protected us. Even in the worst fire we were not hurt, though we were surrounded by it. God was there with us.

> When you walk through the fire,
> you will not be burned;
> the fires will not set you ablaze.
> For I am the LORD, your God,
> the Holy One of Israel, your Saviour...' (Isa. 43: 2b, 3a)

God's healing

At the N'tchumbe Bible Institute I worked as a medic for three years. During high school years, God had directed me to do a two-year course in lab. technology and nutrition. I had also studied both my own and my father's physical problems. Added to this, a senior missionary had shown me how to follow instructions in medical books and so I learnt how to prescribe medicines. Junta, one of the teachers and a mother of two, helped me in many ways especially with the children. We ministered to both villagers and students. I saw the power of the Lord at work. Sometimes we didn't have any appropriate medicine so we prayed against the sickness and the Lord healed. We saw many cases of severe malaria. We treated the patients in their homes but the more serious cases we sent to the hospital, 140 kilometres away.

* * *

One day a student was boiling palm oil in a fifty-five gallon drum. While removing it from the drum, the handle of his bucket broke and the boiling oil poured out over him. It went into his boot and severely burnt his foot. When the boot was removed, the skin came with it. He had third degree burns. Having no medicine, we soaked his foot in water and applied petroleum jelly. I went to Bafata to buy antibiotics and antihistamines. Three weeks later I took him to a doctor in Bissau. The doctor asked how long ago it was since he had been burnt. When we told him he was amazed at the progress he had made.

He was healed in less than a month. To God be the Glory!

* * *

Guinean children are typically breast fed for two years by their mothers who are generally malnourished. The infant mortality rate is high. Sometimes at the age of two the children are too weak to walk. The men and older people eat the meat and vegetables without giving any to the young mothers and children. They often have only the left-over rice to eat. Anaemia, malaria and other diseases hit the three- and four-year-old children hard and many die.

Our Bible School students and workers bring these barely clothed, malnourished children to N'tchumbe and God has put their physical, educational and spiritual needs on my heart. Although our menu is limited, often providing only rice and a small amount of vegetables, we make sure the children eat at a separate table so we can control their diet. Their parents are also learning the need for better nutrition for the children. Two year old Tokna was carried in to us because he was too weak to walk. I supplemented his diet with vegetables and rice and six months later he was running around. I long to be able to provide better food, medicines and clothes for all these children.

* * *

When my house mate, Laureci, needed emergency treatment, she miraculously obtained a visa and an air ticket within one hour to fly to the government hospital in the neighbouring country of Gambia. While there she developed severe cerebral malaria and was in a coma for three days, but God healed her.

* * *

Health has always been my great battle. Most of my life I have suffered from severe headaches, at home, at university and at Bible college. In Africa they were worse, being aggravated by several attacks of malaria and even by the malaria prophylactic medicine that I needed to take. I also suffered a severe attack of sciatica, allergic reactions and intestinal infections, which caused serious weight loss.

I was incapacitated by an injury to my foot. The branch of a large tree fell on my foot and the head of a nail pierced my big toenail, penetrating my toe. For many days I had a high fever. I had to extract the nail and take care of it myself for a week. Some bits of my toenail were left in and caused an infection. I was taken by car to the nearest city, over 50 kilometres away. The doctor wanted to remove my toenail without an anaesthetic. Several friends held me while the doctor used his tweezers. I shouted and told them I could not bear it. So they took me to Bissau where everything was done beautifully.

I suffered many other foot injuries. Running to receive a friend, I slipped on wet cement and broke my right foot. I received good treatment in the hospital in Bissau. Two years later, I twisted my ankle on a loose stone, causing me to fall and fracture my knee. I took the bus to Bissau and then a cab to the hospital. The doctor examined me and sent me to the pharmacist to buy plaster and all that was needed for a cast. I returned to the hospital where the doctor put my foot in a cast but neglected my knee. After two months the cast was removed and I needed physiotherapy but none was available. I suffer from this injury even now; sometimes my knee swells up and is painful. Another time, while running with the children, I fell and sprained my left foot. It was in a cast for a month.

The year 1989-1990 was especially hard, with malaria, a broken leg, an abdominal infection, severe weight loss and an ulcer! I wanted to go home to Brazil and never return. Although it was distressing, I learnt many lessons and I got through victoriously. In Brazil I had studied at a big university and at one of the best Bible Institutes but for my work in Guinea-Bissau I needed other qualifications – patience, humility and love.

A friend in Brazil wrote to encourage me saying: 'Don't worry. God is the one who heals. God can take care of all problems. He can heal malaria, broken bones, abdominal problems… He can remove loneliness. God can give you the ability to speak when you don't have any words. He can give you patience to wait for urgent things. He can give you love when your love runs out. Please stay with your program. You are not alone. The Powerful One is with you.'

God spoke to me through His words to Moses 'I am the LORD who heals you' (Ex. 15:26d). I need doctors to help me but when they are unavailable or reach their limit, I look to the Lord who knows us vastly better than doctors do for He designed and made us. He is present and ready to heal. It is our part to ask and receive. I praise God that I am able to walk normally. In spite of a lifetime of physical problems, I'm able to preach and teach enthusiastically and do all my missionary work even when it requires extensive travel because 'by His wounds we are healed' (Isa. 53:5d).

Forgiveness brings freedom

In 1992, while I was on home leave from Guinea-Bissau, I was invited to speak at a missionary conference in Rio de Janeiro and was asked to give my testimony.

'When I was a toddler I fell out of a high window,' I began, 'and for many years I had psychological problems for which I received treatment and medication. I had problems relating to people. I was diagnosed as autistic. My father was a violent man and harmed us many times at home. I hated him.

'After going through university, no thanks to my father, I went to Bible school. While there the Lord showed me that I could not continue with this hatred in my heart. A visiting missionary preached about forgiveness. She read Matthew 18:21-22 where Jesus told Peter to forgive seventy-seven times. Disturbed in spirit, I went to my dormitory room. The other eleven girls were getting ready for bed. I couldn't control my tears. I just wanted to be alone.

'Our small prayer room was empty, and I went there. I thought of the many times I had been hurt in the past: father, friends, sister, relatives, schoolmates, neighbours, everybody had hurt me. There was a lot of trauma locked up inside me. Even after many years, when I thought of the past, it hurt inside. I asked God, "If I forgive them, could you take the hurt away? It's like my wounds are still bleeding."

'I had already forgiven the others, but my father? I took a piece of paper and listed everything he had done to me. I asked God, "Do I have to forgive everything that he did?" I didn't hear a word, but in my heart I knew I had to. I remembered that three years previously, when my father was dying, he had asked me to forgive him, but the wounds were still bleeding. How could I forgive if it was still hurting? In the small prayer room I cried and cried all night. I didn't want to forgive but I heard the Lord say to me, "If you want to be free, if you want to get rid of all your problems, you have to forgive."

'That was the beginning of everything. He showed me that in order for me to accept myself and others, I had to forgive. "Yes Lord," I said. "I'm going to forgive." On the bottom of that piece of paper where I had listed all that my father had done against me, I wrote, "Father, I forgive you for each of these things, even the worst things, you did to me."

'A great weight lifted from my shoulders. I was free. During the night I prayed to God and was released in my praise to Him. For the first time in my life I sang a song that I had heard on the radio called, "Father you are my hero". After singing, I said, "Father, now I love you" – and I did! After this I wrote to my mother to tell her about this very important day in my life when I forgave my father for all the things he had done to us.'

Yes, we need to forgive to be forgiven and to go free. If I had not forgiven my father at that time, I would not be here today. '

After the service a white woman, a little older than I, stood aside. She caught my eye. 'May I talk to you alone?' she asked. A few minutes later we sat down together in a pew. 'We have a lot in common,' she began.

'Why do you say that?' I asked.

'I, too, had a violent father," she said. 'We were not poor but my father was a drug addict. He did awful things to my family, to me and to my mother. I don't know if it's the same thing that your father did, for which you couldn't forgive him. But I CAN'T forgive my father. It's the first time I'm telling this to anybody. My husband doesn't know. My mother doesn't know. Nobody knows about this. But the Lord said to me while you were speaking that you were the right person to talk to about it. I was raped by my father.' She started crying.

It's not my nature to cry, so even though I felt sorry for her and felt compassion, I didn't cry with her. 'Me too,' I said gently, 'Many times. When I was small and autistic and couldn't defend myself.'

She looked at me and stopped crying. 'So that was what he did to you? You didn't tell us that in church.'

'I don't tell big groups about it because they might start to hate my father. I wouldn't like that because I have forgiven him and the Lord has forgiven him. He has no guilt left on him. There's no need for others to hate him. Can you forgive your father now? If you don't, you will never have victory. You have to tell your husband and pray with him and forgive your father.'

'Before I married,' the woman responded, 'I told my husband that I was not a virgin because a man had raped me. But I never told him who the man was. But there's a difference. My father is still alive.'

'First forgive your father in your heart, then go to him and tell him, "I forgive you for what you did in my life."'

When I had returned to Guinea-Bissau, I received a letter from that lady. She told me what had happened since our meeting: 'Now it's different,' she wrote. 'My husband accepts both me and my father. I went to my father and told him the Lord wanted me to forgive him, and I forgave him totally. He cried a lot. He didn't accept Christ, but he has started going to church.'

Both of us had been bound by past hurts, but as we forgave, Jesus set us free. The wounds were healed, even though the

scars remained.
In all these things we are more than conquerors through him
who loved us. (Rom. 8:37)

Postscript: Autism

My family says that I used to be a very strange girl. Its true. I
could not express myself. I learnt to speak very late. I always
used to find a corner to hide where there were no other people.
In my house I often used to run to a hiding place in a corner of
our restroom. I used to lie on the sofa and fix my eyes on the
ceiling. I might laugh, or start to grunt or shout. I had no friend.
I was always alone. I preferred it that way. I never realised that
I needed anyone else. I had only my sister and my mother as my
defenders. I was autistic.

What is autism? The Autism Society of America has defined
it thus: 'Autism is a severely incapacitating lifelong develop-
mental disability that typically appears during the first three
years of life. The result of a neurological disorder that affects
functioning of the brain, autism and its behavioural symptoms
occur in approximately fifteen out of every 10,000 births.
Autism is four times more common in boys than girls. It has
been found throughout the world in families of all racial, ethnic,
and social backgrounds. No known factors in the psychological
environment of a child have been shown to cause autism.'
(News of ASA, Inc., Jan. – Feb. 1996)

Autism is described as an extreme self-preoccupation usually
accompanied by withdrawal from reality, absorption in fantasy
life, and unrelatedness to other people. Reverie, flights of fancy
and daydreaming are common examples of autistic thinking.
Individuals with autism usually exhibit at least some of the
traits in the following list: difficulty in mixing with other children; insistence on sameness; resistance to changes in routine;
inappropriate laughing and giggling; no fear of dangers; little or
no eye contact; unresponsiveness to normal teaching methods;
prefers to be alone. There are many other symptoms. These
symptoms can range from mild to severe and vary in intensity.
In addition, the behaviour usually occurs across many different
situations and is consistently inappropriate for the age.

I had many of those symptoms. I remember clearly what happened during my childhood because of my habit of doing things many times. I had many problems. One day I was walking from one side to the other of our bedroom and screaming and laughing very loudly. My sister was near me and didn't understand why I was doing that. She started yelling for me to stop. 'Stop ! You're crazy, girl.' She started to shake me and pushed me onto the sofa. I stopped and stared at her, and was there for about three hours without any movement. I was 'absent'.

There are many children who have this problem of autism but I think few of them have recuperated from it as I have. It's very difficult for many people to understand what Jesus did in my life, and they ask 'How can an autistic girl be healed?'

I know God has worked a miracle in my life. It is true that I am still improving in relationship with others, but by His grace God saved and healed me and called me to be a missionary and a teacher. I can speak many languages. I'm invited to many churches to preach. I give seminars in many places, specially in Bible schools. He has set me free!

To Him be all the glory.

Liz

God's interfering presence

What's in a name?

His mother died in childbirth. The man bent down and tenderly gathered the slippery newborn into his arms. To that orphaned lamb the farmer gave the name Philip. A child was also born to the farmer that same day, a daughter. He gave her the name Elizabeth. Philip and Elizabeth – it was 1953, the year of Queen Elizabeth's coronation. Being royalists, the Australian farmer and his wife paid a double tribute to the Commonwealth monarchy that day. Philip was not destined to become lamb chops – pet lambs became a part of the family and died of old age.

And what of Elizabeth's destiny? My name, Elizabeth, means 'dedicated to God' or 'house of God'. I was named by a nominal Christian mother and an agnostic father. Their firstborn daughter consecrated to God by virtue of the name given to her. Time would reveal the prophetic nature of that name.

Farm and small town life were idyllic. Our neighbour, Mr Rosser, was about 110 years old, or at least that is what we thought. His weather-beaten, basset-hound face peeped out from underneath an equally weather-beaten and battered hat. Every morning he set out in his horse-drawn sulky to check his rabbit traps. And every afternoon he would come to a halt outside our modest rented weatherboard house at number 18 Molong Street, Molong. My big brother, two-and-a-half years my senior, helped me to climb up into the sulky. Then little sister was hauled up. Baby brother came next. He never seemed to mind when we accidentally dropped him on his head.

Our daily adventure began – the ride to Mr Rosser's house at number 26. Spinster daughter Edna warmly greeted us, and then kept a watchful eye as we headed for the swings in their backyard. We swung higher, higher, straining to see the wheat silos and train line down the bottom of the hill, and the creek beyond that. Higher, higher. It was exactly the same every day. A time to swing then 'Home you go!' Edna called, and so we began to meander home, past the stone Cobb & Co stables with the fresh smell of horse manure, our bare feet toughened by the dirt and pebbles of the footpath.

It never dawned on us that the reason we rarely wore shoes was because Mum and Dad could not afford them. We did have one pair each, but they were only to be worn on special occasions, like to school and to Sunday School. Even when we played in the paddock at the back of our house we did not wear shoes. 'Cathead' burrs really stung if we trod on them. So we ripped old cardboard boxes into pieces and placed them strategically on the ground. We used the pieces as stepping-stones and soon we were shooting from one side of the paddock to the other as we revelled in games of cowboys and Indians and World War II combat troops hiding in an old bunker.

Hospital and heroines

At Sunday School dear jolly, roly-poly-shaped Mrs Bath taught us about the missionary journeys of St Paul. Then there were the Bible memory verses. The unfamiliar 'thees' and 'thous' had me tripping over my tongue at times, but I loved Mrs Bath and I was determined to excel with those memory verses. Early Sunday mornings I would lie in bed reciting the verses for the thousandth time just to be sure I knew them word perfectly. Mrs Bath was very kind. She smiled a lot. Was she Mrs God? She could give hugs, something God could not do.

At eight years old I devoured a children's version of Gladys Aylward's story. This little English missionary became my heroine. What adventure, what courage! I even forfeited play time during recess at school and sat poring over the pages with my mind and heart soaring to China. It was as if I, too, were part of the band of children trudging with Miss Aylward over rugged mountain ranges and fording rushing streams. The bed bugs and head lice were formidable enemies but the real enemy was even more fearsome. No, we were not going to be caught by the invading Chinese army. Our God would deliver us! Our God? Ironically, I knew very little about God.

Hospital! Oh the pain! My left ankle throbbed. The pain

intensified. I could not tolerate moving the leg, let alone have someone touch it. I was wafting in and out of consciousness. 'I want my Mummy.' Tears. Pain. Noise. Blurred faces peering down at me. 'Osteomyelitis,' I heard. Night and day merged, weeks...

One morning I woke up. I was hungry – alive. The doctors had operated on my ankle and it was slowly healing. But they feared the condition had recurred and so extended my time in hospital. I was a big girl now, aged ten, and My Favourite Nurse allowed me to stay up late when the little kids had to go to sleep. She and I sneaked off to another room and she thrilled me with stories of Jesus and of her plans to become a missionary. Now I had two heroines, Miss Aylward and My Favourite Nurse. I, too, would become a missionary.

God's pursuing presence

The prophetic name

I drifted through my childhood with a somewhat hit-and-miss religious exposure. The late 1960s arrived. As far as I was concerned, God could stay floating up above the clouds some place and I would stay below the clouds and do whatever I liked. After all, God was some unknowable mass of something or other who would not or could not possibly be involved with what was happening on the ground. We were all living in a Yellow Submarine listening to Sergeant Pepper's Lonely Heart's Club Band. And My Sweet Lord Krishna was just around the corner.

In my one desire to be liked and get invited to the 'right' parties, I embraced the Beatles, the Monkees, the Bee Gees and ABBA – oh such a struggle to stay in the 'in crowd'.

As a vulnerable, almost-17-year-old country kid, I made my way to Sydney. There I encountered marijuana and gurus, 'making love not war', barefoot, long-haired Jesus freaks, Hell's Angels, the Children of God, the post World War II baby-boomers coming of age in their rebellion – what a smorgasbord.

Elizabeth – consecrated to God. Did I have a choice? It seemed not. I began my general nursing training, housed in a four-storey nurses' residence. Who arranged for me to be on a corridor surrounded by Christians? My vulnerability responded to the genuine love and care shown to me by a number of these Christian nurses. I attended an evangelical church for the first time in my life. God began to come down from above the clouds. I wrote home and asked my parents to send me the Bible that I had been given at Sunday School. They were very surprised. I began to read that Bible, devour it in fact. It was now making sense. God showed up. He smiled. I smiled. We embraced. Now I knew to whom I belonged. I understood.

My friends, like me, were trainee nurses. Many were Christians. I was a Christian now. They wanted to become missionaries. Surely the most logical thing in the world was that I, too, became a missionary.

One of the pastors was a former missionary to India. The Nurses' Christian Fellowship had a strong missions emphasis. I got involved in missions prayer groups. We lived near a missionary training college. I was discovering that God is an expert at setting things up. He was bombarding me with exposure to cross-cultural missions.

Is God clever?

I began to pray that my parents would become Christians, but I gave up after a while because God was not answering. In fact, things became worse. Dad thought I had gone 'overboard' and he was not impressed with my plans to become a missionary and, in his view, 'ditch' nursing.

My 40-plus-years Mum shocked me with news one day. She and Dad were expecting another baby! It seemed that their shock was even greater than that of mine and my siblings. 'Little Kid' became a hit. A sister tacked on right down there at the end was a delight.

Two years later Mum sat me down again. She had something very important to say. 'Oh no! Not pregnant again!' My siblings and I could cope – could our parents? But I was wrong. My Mum was not pregnant, rather she had become a Christian! It happened on 16 May 1973, three years to the very day after I had met God myself. Coincidence? I think not. The Shepherd spoke: 'See, I heard your prayers and just to prove it, I gave both you and your mother the same re-birthday.' Is God clever, or what?

Take delight in the Lord

Midwifery training followed my general nurse training. Being a gung-ho, extrovert type, I quickly found myself in leadership positions of the Nurses' Christian Fellowship. Nurse training was teaching me more than anatomy and physiology. I learnt planning, administration, and interpersonal skills, and about team membership and leadership.

Nor did the spiritual status quo satisfy me. I wanted to know God. I read of hunger and thirst for God and went in hot pursuit of Him. Or did He come in hot pursuit of me?

I fell into bed after night duty, the recently arrived letter lying open on the floor. It was asking me if I was serious about committing myself to long-term missionary work. Was I prepared to really do that? I tossed and turned, tired after a heavy night at work. Thoughts bounced off each other. Was Jesus really Lord of my life? That was the bottom line. Hour after hour. No sleep came. What would I have to give up? Did He really know what He was doing? Could He be trusted? Would He take all the freedom and fun out of my life?

Was the will of God good, acceptable and perfect as the apostle Paul had written in Romans 12? Or was it bad, unacceptable and far from perfect?

Finally: 'I would be a fool to turn my back on You. You are my Lord.' I slept like a baby.

It was New Year's Eve. My pastor began to speak about Psalm 37:4: ''Take delight in the Lord and He will give you the desires of your heart.' That sermon was for me. And that verse became my life's verse. 'Delight in the Lord, be consumed with Him, focus on Him,' he said. 'Your desires will therefore line up with God's desires,' he explained. 'Then He can give you the desires of your heart because they are exactly the same as His desires.'

God's abiding presence

Missionary training

One chilly but blue-skied sunny afternoon in May 1975 I shifted down a gear and guided the car along the driveway of the WEC

(Worldwide Evangelization for Christ) Missionary Training College in Launceston, Tasmania. I drove slowly, wondering if I should turn around and hightail it out of there! Was I ready for this? It was so unknown. Scary. To train and depart for Spain as a missionary – my goal. I kept driving and pulled into the car park.

Two vivid years followed. I remember...theology classes, struggling to get my brain around the concept...picnics at the river on a Saturday afternoon...forging friendships that would last through the years...eyeing off the guys wondering if I would marry one of them...being petrified about preaching classes. I remember sitting in a tree in the paddock below the lecture hall and practising my sermon on the cows. They were so impressed.

I remember letting off steam late at night grabbing pillows and dashing off on 'dorm raids'. That is inevitably what happens when a bunch of girls in their early twenties live in confined spaces! What fun to have pillows flying, bodies rolling on the floor, peals of laughter echoing along the corridors.

Then there was the day the Principal publicly asked his Deputy for forgiveness. That led to many, staff and students alike, asking each other for forgiveness. This was the real missionary training, I thought, more than the classroom stuff.

I can vividly recall our first official 'day of prayer'. How on earth was I going to pray for a whole day? Surely this stuff was reserved for the desert fathers, the saints of old? Wouldn't it be easier to spend the day digging ditches? Did prayer actually do anything, anyway? I knew it was supposed to, I even agreed that it was supposed to, but did it, really?

And I remember staff members who fell on their knees and prayed their hearts out for the students, including me.

I also remember the restlessness as I tried to come to terms with my inferiority complex. With time on my hands at weekends I would jump in the car and go to the shopping mall, only to be confronted with myself there yet again. Then back into the car to find another location, and still I accompanied myself. I remember staff members who listened, counselled, prayed. I remember the children's song that I taught to a group of seven-year-olds at a local school during the weekly religious instruction classes: 'And I just thank You, Father, for making me, me.' Somehow my Heavenly Father firmly convinced me, deep within, that I, too, was being talked about in Psalm 139. He had chosen to make me, me.

Finally I remember Graduation Day, May 1977. I stood on the platform with the other graduating students. We were each given just one minute to sum up the most important lesson we had learned during our training. Mine took only ten seconds. 'Now I know that my Heavenly Father loves me.' It had not happened through formal lectures. Those who had watched it unfold knew the path I had come. They knew of the coming to an experiential realisation that I was made exactly as I was because God had chosen it that way, He planned it that way, He wanted it that way. I had not somehow slipped into the human race when God was not looking. He loved me.

'I was not disobedient to the vision from heaven' was the text of the graduation address. There are few sermons I remember beyond a few hours, but that one stuck. Burned into my soul, in fact. Obedience did not seem to be a burden now. The graduating group of students sang a chorus that was based on Romans 12:1,2, 'I give myself to You as a living sacrifice, holy and acceptable to God.'

The staff had prayed and asked God for the Bible verse that would be given to me along with my certificate. 'And without faith it is impossible to please God, because anyone who comes to him must believe that he exists and that he rewards those who earnestly seek him' (Heb. 11:6). At times during my missionary career that verse has jumped to conscious memory. Yes, there have been times when I wondered if God was there at all. Then, I needed to work through from the beginning: what is the evidence? There have also been times when I have found myself being wooed by God, and found myself with an insatiable desire to seek Him, to know Him.

Viva Espana!

'Lord, I want to go to Spain as a missionary. If you do not want me there, then stop me.' He never did. I went. Now, what had brought that on?

'Only 2% of the world's missionary force work in Europe,' he told us. Different missionary speakers at church had brought Europe into focus for me. 'Spain is a needy mission field,' another asserted.

May 1979 saw my arrival at Madrid Barajas airport. My missionary career had begun in earnest. Kind of. I wasn't sure if I was a missionary or just culture shocked, feeling spiritually inadequate, and insecure.

A tall, blonde Australian is a sharp contrast to short, dark Spaniards. Some older Spanish ladies were so short that even when I sat down I was still taller than they were! Blonde foreign girls did not have a good reputation in Spain. Men would talk to me on the street and I felt very vulnerable. I wanted to hide. The food was so different, too, and I ate so many olives during my first few weeks that I would retch even driving past an olive grove! And in language study I encountered verb conjugations – it seemed there were more exceptions to the rule than there were regular verbs.

Was this intensity of homesickness normal? Anguish tore at my heart and leaked out my eyeballs. I was afraid to appear a failure, and I withdrew from others. Some days I couldn't cope with the language course, so I left classes early and sat in McDonald's waiting for the time for classes to end, then returned home – attempting to deceive my flatmate into thinking I'd had a wonderful day at language school. On a few occasions I did the same where church was concerned. I sat alone on a park bench, wallowing in self-pity while others sang and clapped and had a jolly old time at church. I couldn't face it. I was a failure, withdrawn, depressed, hiding.

After about a year living in Spain I finally admitted to myself that I needed help. I felt down in the dumps, that I was not up to par with those other WECers. I could not go home to Australia as my pride would not allow me to admit I had failed. I could not stay in Spain. Should I simply disappear – take my toothbrush and run? But where to? Maybe I had demonic problems, and a good dose of deliverance would be the thing? Some caring team members arranged for me to see a visiting English pastor and his wife. The tap was turned on, out flowed my jumbled story, and they listened.

Finally, the wife looked at me and said, 'We know what the real issue is. You need to fall in love with Jesus.' 'But I am already a Christian!' I blurted. 'Yes, we know. That is not what we're saying.'

In hindsight, they were right. Their prayer was simple enough: 'Let Liz fall in love with You. Amen.' Over twenty years

down the track, all I can say is they were bang on. They were
talking about devotion and passion, about loving the Lord with
all my heart, not just a cold, remote, intellectual understanding
of Him.

An end came to culture shock. Passion for Jesus grew. Love
for Spain, the language, the paella and tortilla increased. I was
out and about, building friendships, settling in. My niche was
found.

God at work

'What does a missionary in Madrid do?' was a question that I
was often asked by folk back home. 'Church planting' seems
such a grandiose term. 'Hang around with people talking to
them about Jesus' seemed the most accurate answer. The 'hanging around' meant going where the people were – to the parks,
the sidewalk cafes, the plazas, the shopping centres. Heroin
addicts were often the ones most open to listen to the Gospel.

How does one approach a Spaniard, traditionally a Roman
Catholic, in practice a secularist or materialist? What a rich history – seven hundred years of occupation by the Moors, the
architecture, the Inquisition, King Ferdinand and Queen Isabel
sending Christopher Columbus across the ocean blue, world
conquests, the sending out of priests as missionaries. Who was
I to come to their country as a missionary? Did I consider them
to be pagans? Barbarians? Unconverted? Lessons in servant-
hood were forthcoming.

Was I God's answer for Spain? Or was Spain God's answer
for me? A veteran missionary once said to me, 'When you come
to the mission field all the dregs in your life rise to the surface.'
Selfish attitudes bubbled up. Anger erupted. Not a pretty picture. People at home in Australia had stood me on a pedestal
with its accompanying plaque 'our missionary'. But I knew the
sinful truth. The refining process stripped away the self-right-
eous veneer and headed for the interior.

Hang the sex

'Hang the sex, I just want someone to hang the curtains!' I
exploded one day. No, that is not a book title, but it may well
become one! Life as a single lady missionary could at times be

burdensome. It wasn't so much the living with my sexuality that was the struggle, but rather the day-by-day issues. What was I supposed to be anyway? Plumber, carpenter, negotiator with electricity, gas and telephone companies, driller, curtain hanger, electrician – the latter came to an abrupt halt one day when I accidentally allowed two live wires to touch and my brain was fried and my hair permed all in one split second! A husband would have come in very handy for all these odd jobs.

Well into my twenties I figured that if I hit thirty and was not married I would be devastated, the universe would cave in. The brunt of jokes – being left on the shelf. My thirtieth birthday arrived and still there was no eligible bachelor in sight. Surprise, surprise, I did not self-destruct! I rather fancied that I took on an air of maturity. As one friend quipped, 'like old cheese!' Heading for forty I found myself enjoying being single. I was challenged with the question, 'If the Lord wants you to get married, are you prepared to do so?' What a change. I found I wasn't. I enjoyed my freedom, basically doing what I wanted and going where I wanted. Was I prepared to submit myself in love to someone forever? Whoa, heady stuff.

God's forgiving presence

To forgive or not to forgive, that is the question

November 1982 is etched in my memory. The damp, dark winter sky hung low, enveloping Kent, England. Having grown up in sunny country Australia, and usually living in sunny central Spain, this was indeed miserable weather.

Some friends had taken me into their home for a few days of rest and recuperation. What bliss. Walks by the sea, despite the windy and chilly weather. Piping hot cups of strong English tea. Love expressed. Warm fuzzies. Peace.

Over a bedtime drink my friends looked at me with smiles that reflected wisdom. 'Why not take some time to be quiet with the Lord, Liz? Stay in your room tomorrow. Ask Him if He has anything to say to you. Reflect on your time in Spain. Let Him do the talking. You be quiet.' Now, this was something new for me, your compulsive activist whose prayer life consisted of long lists and much talking. But this idea of listening to God...well,

'I'll give it a go,' I gingerly replied.

A new day dawned, more dark clouds and fog. This was my day to listen to God. Still feeling rather proud of myself for having learned Spanish, overcome culture shock, and discipled new converts, the picture of success, I crawled out of bed to start my listening.

Blow me down if I wasn't surprised by the first thing God said!

'Why do you call me "Lord, Lord," and do not do what I say?'

Surely He didn't mean me. After all, I had obeyed His missionary call and gone to Spain. That was at some sacrifice I'll hasten to add. I had given up a good nursing career. I had left family, friends and country. I had even survived without Vegemite!

'Why do you call me "Lord, Lord," and do not do what I say?'

I had…I had…I had not forgiven when hurt. I had blamed others for making my life miserable. I had harboured resentment in my heart. I had kindled that resentment until it became a root of bitterness. I had lain in bed at night, unable to sleep, and churned the resentment around in my stomach inventing conversations in which I rebuked and condemned others. But did I confront them face-to-face? Never! These were not dirty rotten sinners I was hitting out at – these were my missionary co-workers! I had called Him 'Lord, Lord' and not done what He told me to do.

Unforgiveness had become like a big ball of barbed wire inside my stomach. The slightest movement caused the barbs to jab. Ouch! Unforgiveness had found expression in barbed comments about others. It ate away at me, agitating, thrashing. I had held onto reactions that in turn had bound me up inside.

Turning to Luke 6, I pondered verses 37 and 46: 'Do not judge. Forgive, and you will be forgiven.' My heart was exposed. It was stony, cold, hard. I had judged others. I had failed to forgive. But, they had hurt me. Why was I the one that ended up with the problem? In the midst of trying to justify my position, my defences crumbled. I had failed to be open. I had failed to support those whom the Lord had sent to be my co-workers.

Slowly, deliberately, I expressed forgiveness to the Lord. 'Now pray for them,' the Voice said. What? Hurts from the past threatened to bind me up again. 'How can I pray for them when they have done this to me?' Fortunately I recognised the subtle tactics of the enemy who was so quickly trying to rob me of inner freedom. I began to pray. 'Now get on your knees as a sign of submission to me,' the Lord challenged. Down I went and poured out my heart on behalf of my co-workers whom I now saw as dear not only to the Lord but also to me.

Forgiveness means to release another from judgment. I had indeed stood in judgment of others. That day I was confronted with a choice. Feeling somewhat hemmed into a corner by the Lord, I made my decision. Yes, I would forgive. It slowly dawned on me that it was in fact I who had caused many of my own problems, simply by clamming up and being too self-protective to talk openly with my colleagues. To release someone from judgment brought tremendous freedom. No longer would that resentment rule my life.

A couple of weeks later I found myself back in Australia, shut away for the day to continue the forgiveness process. (I was prepared to stay longer if that's what it took.) Out came a big sheet of paper. 'Lord, who else do I need to forgive?' Down went the names, one after the other. Tears coursed down my face as I remembered the pain that some of these people had inflicted upon me. That day I chose to forgive, and told the Lord so.

Two of the names stared back at me as I peered at my list. These were ones it was impossible to forgive. The pain was too great, the damage too deep.

A number of days later an older Christian friend who had become somewhat of a mentor to me sat beside me on the river bank. I could smell gum trees. Pink and white galahs chattered with white cockatoos in the branches overhead. 'I cannot forgive,' I blurted out. My wise friend drew breath and quietly admonished, 'The word is not cannot. It is will not.' My heart raced. The adrenaline pumped. 'I have my rights! They hurt me! I was the innocent party!'

'Do you choose to forgive?' came her gentle yet firm reply. Here was a choice that would mean release from bitterness, or perpetual inner turmoil and a missionary life that would be continually hampered by the fact that I was refusing to do what God had told me to do. A battle raged in my heart. My friend said no more. Time ticked slowly by. Yes, I would choose to forgive. I did not feel like it, but I made a deliberate choice with my will.

To this day, one of the people that I struggled to forgive knows nothing of that battle at the river bank. Others have remarked that this man took on a sudden spurt of growth as a Christian from that time on. A coincidence? I don't think so. He was released from judgment and therefore was free to grow.

And they all lived happily ever after? Don't you believe it! Unforgiveness/resentment is my area of weakness. The potential is there for me to be bound up by it again, and to bind others up in the process. Reconciliation is the message that threads its way through the whole Bible. Matt. 5:23,24 and Matt. 18:15 both speak on the issue. Whether I know someone has something against me, or I have something against them, the responsibility is on me to go and talk openly – not attackingly, not defensively, but humbly. From time to time seemingly small issues become a big deal and I am hurt. What I do with that hurt is my responsibility. I am the one who can turn the situation into one that is sweet through forgiving, or I can keep it sour.

God's compassionate presence

The missionary

So – back in Spain – I was a missionary…I think…

…Comforting a distraught, grieving mother whose eighteen-year-old daughter Maria lay on a cold slab in a morgue. Her life cut short by heroin abuse and then finalised by a fatal car accident.

…Isabel's parents were extremely angry that she had aligned herself with evangelicals. Often they did not allow her to attend church. Certainly they would not have me visit their home. How to disciple Isabel? Two or three afternoons each week I met her outside the shop where she worked. We spent about 20 minutes talking flat out as we walked around the block. We would talk through a number of issues relating to life with Jesus, and then she would head towards the entrance of her apartment block lest her mother begin to wonder what took her so long to get home from work.

Patricia

At the end of 1987 I left Spain to begin a new ministry. For the six months before my departure, I grieved. This had indeed become my home. This was my land, my country, my people.

On my last day in Madrid, Patricia and I ate breakfast together in a bar and revisited where she had come from. There was that first phone call she ever made to me 'Are you the missionary?' 'Yes, I am'. 'Well I am a drug addict and missionaries are supposed to help drug addicts. Meet me in the plaza in twenty minutes!' I had put the phone down, dazed.

Her story had unfolded. Her father was dead. Her mother lived locally. Patricia's legs showed scars from her attempt to commit suicide by jumping from a third-storey window. She had spent months in traction in hospital. She wanted to get off drugs. Off she went to a rehabilitation centre and there she met Jesus.

And there we sat, facing each other over steaming breakfast coffee and piping hot croissants. We remembered the day I went to a lawyer on her behalf. The day I accompanied her to court. How ridiculous it sounded: 'The accused is found guilty of robbing a bar-owner at fork-point.' Not even a gun, not even a knife, but a fork!

Patricia was different now. Free of heroin, a restored relationship with her mother, her soul undergoing a transformation process, and sorting out her sexual orientation. She was baptised, an up-and-coming leader of an apartment that took in heroin addicts for rehabilitation. My last day as a missionary in Spain. It had been worth it. Just to see Patricia's radiant face and hear her talk of her big God. Yes, it had all been worth it.

About two years later, the letter lay on my desk in the Netherlands. 'Two police officers peered through the smashed window of the abandoned car,' it said. 'The hypodermic still in her arm. Dead.' Just another junkie? No, this was Patricia. 'No!', I screamed, 'How was this possible?' My mind went back to that breakfast. What happened? Her anger had proved to be her downfall. A seemingly trivial matter had exploded into unmanageable proportions and Patricia had stormed out. The old self-hatred had resurfaced – and her mind began to crave heroin again.

Why? My reactions swung from anger to a sense of helplessness. A life wasted? A ploy of the enemy? Did Patricia really belong to the Lord? Is she in heaven? My tidy pages of theology were all ripped up.

All we do is train missionaries

May 3, 1989 the plane winged its way down over neatly formed, green fields that were crisscrossed by small canals with neat matchbox houses dotted here and there. 'Welcome to Amsterdam' the sign at the airport read. I was moving to the Netherlands to be part of the founding faculty of WEC's European Missionary Training College. I brought along a deep desire to be involved in training others to reach the unreached, one year of staff training at the WEC Missionary Training College in Tasmania, and a Master's degree in Missiology 20% completed.

During my last couple of years in Spain a number of the new Christian young people were asking for more in-depth Bible study. Some were asking about cross-cultural missions and reading missionary biographies. To be with these young people was so refreshing. They were hungry. Then the WEC leadership began discussing starting a missionary training college in Europe. 'Was this something for me?' I wondered. I let the thought sit in my heart for a number of months. Then I consulted leadership of both church and mission, those who knew me well. Could they see that this was indeed the Lord's path for me? There was a resounding 'Yes.' I found that accountability and counsel go a long way. Somehow it is safe. Those around me help to keep me from stepping over the edge into something absurd.

'I've seen Jesus in you when you're up but what has made the most impact on my life is that I have seen Jesus in you when you are down,' Susanna confided in her inimitable gentle style. Missionary training – it is sharing our lives, empowering students to grow, rolling with them through the ups and downs of life and the dealings of the Lord, tutoring those who struggled with writing essays, listening not just to their words but to their hearts, praying them through to better places.

Graduation days have to be among my favourites. Students stand on that platform recounting their stories. As expected, most of what they learned was in the non-formal and informal settings. In a sense no-one cares what grades they achieved or what essays they wrote. This is a day to recall, to reflect on those encounters with God, to ponder those deep inner struggles with their pasts that had jumped up to meet them. To revel in the times when God let the bottom fall out of heaven and we prayed with all our hearts for Muslims to be saved. To gaze in wonder at the Word as a particular passage suddenly made sense.

And there is the cross-cultural rub and enrichment – lives and rooms shared with those from a completely different culture. I sit. I listen. I watch. This is the stuff of which real missionaries are made. Sadly, there are also those who have the 'right' words, but lack the breaking and depth that the Holy Spirit works in people. Have we as a staff failed them? Have we prayed enough? Have we listened to them? Have we challenged them enough?

The Gen-X mystic

'Generation X' they are called. A frustration, or potential? Why do they seem to find it so difficult to commit themselves long term to anything? The Voice spoke, 'This is my chosen generation. These are my missionaries in the making.' Yes, such potential! They would not let me get away with any clichés or glib answers. How does it work? Does it work for you? Is it true in your own life? A threat? Or a challenge?

We sat in the pancake restaurant, the Gen-X mystic, his fiancée and me. 'Teach us to dangle the feet of our soul,' the Gen-X mystic prayed as we sat at the table. Now that was some variant on grace before a meal! Some prayers make you sit up and listen. I listened. A quest for depth in my life reached up and took hold of my soul. Who was training whom here? I dangled my feet. I ate pancakes.

Doing Church in a brothel

Perched precariously on a rickety stool I stretched on tiptoe reaching, up, up. Was this really part of world evangelisation? We had been walking through the Red Light district, as was our custom, greeting the women who worked 'behind the windows'. This was Arnhem, made famous by the World War II film 'A Bridge Too Far'. I regularly travelled over the John Frost Bridge that featured in the film. John Frost was an American soldier who had bravely tried to keep the advancing Germans at bay on that bridge. Within a stone's throw of the celebrated bridge lay the infamous Red Light district, glory and shame side by side. And so to that evening and the stool.

Pamela rushed out calling for me to come into her room. 'I have been waiting days for you to come.' At last, a soul ready to accept Jesus! Or so I thought. 'My coloured light bulbs are blown. You are the only person I know who is tall enough to change them.' And so I stretched, reaching up to change those light bulbs in the sockets of that extremely high ceiling.

My mind wandered back to my first encounter with Pamela. In fact, my mind drifted back to why I came to the Red Light district in the first place. 'Liz, we need a Spanish-speaking person and you are it!' declared one of the missionary training college students who had visited the women in prostitution. Around eighty percent were native Spanish speakers, and very few spoke any Dutch or English.

Spanish is one of those languages that is spoken not just with the mouth, but from the depths of one's being, and with much Latin animation thrown in for good measure. Once again I enjoyed being able to use *el idioma de los cielos* (the language of heaven).

A few months after I became a regular member of this all-women outreach team, I was strolling past a particular brothel one evening when an unusually short Dutch girl with a booming voice yelled at me, 'How dare you come here! Go away! We don't want you! We don't want your religion!'

'Fine!', I thought, 'That's it! You don't want me, so I can't be bothered with you either! I will go away and I won't come back!' I felt deeply hurt and intimidated. How dare she give me a hard time? How dare she threaten me!

My co-worker took me for a coffee. 'Liz, do you come here because you have a deep compassion for these women, or do you come because you enjoy the opportunity to speak Spanish?'

Thump! I did not have a compassionate bone in my body towards these women. I came purely because I enjoyed the opportunity to speak Spanish. My friend exhorted, 'I suggest you do not come back unless you come with more pure motives.'

'Lord, give me Your heart for the broken, the hurting,' I prayed. What happened? Within a few short weeks I found myself with a very different attitude. My heart was becoming linked to their hearts. Their pain was becoming my pain. The God of all compassion had come.

* * *

Christine and I sat side by side on her bed. 'I'm tired. I'm going home to my own country. I have had enough.' We had talked together over the months. She had come to a special dinner. As the *Jesus* film was shown one of her friends excitedly exclaimed, 'Hey, look! Jesus hung around with women like us!' I caught a glimpse of Christine, tears rolling down her face. And there we sat. 'Christine, Jesus forgives you.' She laid her head on my shoulder and wept – tears of release as she accepted his forgiveness. My colleague and I wept also.

* * *

We sat around the big table in the kitchen at the back of one of the brothels. My Spanish co-worker and I loved these times at what we affectionately termed *La iglesia de la cocina* (the church of the kitchen). I'm sure Jesus was there, too. We were immersed in Luke's Gospel when one of the pimps stuck his head in the door. I tensed. These were tricky times. Would he allow us to continue? After all, it was 'work' time for his 'charges'.

'Everything all right, girls?'

'*Si!*' came the collective reply, and he left.

On to the next verse. A potential client wandered in and was told to come back after the Bible study.

To sing with those ladies was no staid affair. How can a Latina possibly sing without dancing? 'Hey, this is like church,' pronounced one lady, 'so we need to take up an offering!' An offering? An offering of money gained from prostitution services? Was this acceptable to God? But then came, 'Liz, you are our pastor, so we want you to have the offering.' My mind went into an ethical, moral spin. To reject their money would be synonymous with rejecting them. I accepted the offering, and later discreetly slipped the money into our team's literature fund.

* * *

The mobile phone rang. Julie answered. It was her mother, an evangelical calling from her home country.

'Mum, I'm at a Bible study at the moment.' What the mother did not know was that we were sitting on her daughter's bed, a bed used for prostitution; but in truth, we were reading the Bible together and would soon kneel beside that same bed and ask God to help her two children back in the home country. How many lies had Julie's mother been told? Of work in a factory, of happiness?

* * *

'Let's celebrate our birthdays together!' exclaimed one of the ladies. Five of us had birthdays within 6 weeks of each other. My co-worker and I drove to the prearranged meeting point. These three ladies were among those to whom we were closest. Anita and I looked forward to celebrating in a normal environment instead of the usual brothel where we visited them. The restaurant setting was picturesque, on the edge of town, and overlooking the tree-lined river with its inevitable stream of barges. Yet something was wrong. All three ladies swung from being very giggly to becoming angry. Drugs? Alcohol? A combination of both? It was like being out with three people we didn't know. We ate, we drove them back to work and dropped them off. Anita and I felt totally let down, confused, despairing. Our hearts were heavy. What went wrong? We sat side by side in the car, not speaking.

* * *

Why do I tell these stories? In many ways I do not want to tell them. I do not want the lives of these women to be used for sensational purposes, or sadly, as a brunt of jokes. These are my friends. (I've changed their names for this book).

Exploitation is at the heart of prostitution. I wonder if it is possible to write about them without exploiting them further?

These are women with deep wounds. Most of the ladies have been emotionally manipulated, or psychologically manoeuvred, or forced physically into prostitution. Usually all three. Many have suffered childhood sexual abuse, mainly from men but also from women. Their lives are caught up in blackmail and deception, their pain deadened with alcohol and drugs. Yet they are ladies who have been made in the image of God, made to be worshippers of their Creator.

After watching consistent abuse we, as an outreach team, cry out 'Enough!' Half of us are the pray-ers, the other half are the workers on the street. We need each other. Each of us can react or respond in different ways. We get angry with the pimps, at the clients. The abuse can crush our hearts. Our view of sexuality can be thrown off balance. We confess our vulnerability to each other. We protect each other, not just physically but also emotionally and spiritually. We never go out onto the streets without our prayer team backing us up with intercession.

The problem is not in what these women in prostitution do, it is in what they become. Prostitution damages physical health but it goes much deeper than that. As Julie once candidly admitted to me, 'This work is destroying my soul.' How does one help someone rebuild her soul? Sometimes I wonder if I know. What we as a team do know is that genuine love, friendship, and respect speak volumes.

My mind wandered to Mary of Egypt. In the fifth century twelve-year-old Mary ran away to Alexandria and became a prostitute. Something about Jerusalem drew her to that city. To pay her passage she offered her sexual services to the crew of the ship. Upon arrival in Jerusalem she continued to work in prostitution. Then God came and she heard the Voice say, 'Cross over the Jordan and you will find rest.' She crossed. God found her and she found God. And the next 47 years until her death in the desert were spent discovering the depths of God. What does it take for an Arnhem lady to discover God and be transformed in the depths of her soul? Yes, they want us to pray and read the Bible, yes they are glad we visit, yes they appreciate the Bibles and other literature we give them, and yet very few cross over the Jordan and stay there.

At one time it really disturbed me that I lived in a Christian community at the missionary training college, yet did not seem to be out there 'doing' evangelism at the front line of the mission field, out there in the wilds of Central Asia or some such far-flung place. Then up came the names of my friends in Arnhem. The Voice spoke, 'These are the ones I have given you.' I knew. It was staring me in the face. The Arnhem Red Light district was my place of 'being' evangelism.

Ask, plead, weep

Heaven. Older brother (aged around 8 years at the time) expounded the characteristics of heaven to me. He was an expert on all things: snakes, beetles and bugs, kangaroos, wombats, emus, catching crayfish – and heaven.

Revelation 7:9 gives a somewhat more accurate picture than that of my brother. At times when I pray I begin to 'see' it. Cheering and clapping on the streets as I watch the delight on Jesus' face as representatives from every tribe, tongue and nation arrive. His Father had said to Him, 'Ask of me and I will give you the nations as your inheritance' (Psalm 2:8). And Jesus asked His Father. And I also ask. And the Father will do it.

There was a time when prayer did not work, or so it seemed. And yet there was a haunting something that told me to keep pursuing and I would know. What was it about those biographies of praying people? Moses, daringly staring God in the face and telling Him that He could not do what He had threatened to do (Exod. 32)? Epaphras agonising in prayer (Col. 4:12)? In the Old Testament, Jewish leaders failed to pray. Goodness, could some praying have stopped God's wrath being poured out and saved those people from being consumed with fiery anger (Ezek. 22:30,31)? Gosh, all that sobering responsibility – scary thought.

Prayer dribbled into my life, drop by drop until it became an unstoppable stream. It moved from a 'nice chat with God' to an awe-inspiring privilege and responsibility.

Years ago a somewhat shy and unremarkable fellow-WECer came to the Netherlands on a visit. That visit was to upset my lifestyle greatly! Tuesday afternoons equalled missionary prayer meeting. Oh such dull, uninteresting, boring times. A one and a half hour's endurance test. Find any legitimate excuse not to attend those compulsory meetings.

Shy, unremarkable WECer challenged, 'Liz, I want you to pray that Tuesday afternoon missionary prayer meetings become the highlight of the college week.' Asking the impossible. Get real woman! I confessed, 'These afternoons are a grind to me. They are certainly not the highlight of my week. Perhaps I should start there.' 'Lord, I pray that Tuesday afternoon missionary prayer times will become the highlight of my week. Amen.' Within one semester God answered. Blow me away! How does He do that? Praying became exciting. Leading and mentoring others in prayer became a passion with me. To enforce in prayer what Jesus had achieved through the cross and the resurrection was right up my alley.

I believed the Lord was asking me to 'adopt' the Kazaks as a prayer focus. Oh to see Folk Islam crumble in the lives of Kazaks, and for the Gospel to penetrate those held for so long in deception. God is doing it!

Suddenly one day I came face to face with Tibetan Buddhism. A photo of a pilgrim prostrating herself before the Jokhang temple in Lhasa ('the place of gods'), the capital of Tibet, gripped my heart. It seemed to me that with every prostration these pilgrims were reinforcing their bondage. The Tibetans wiggled their way under my skin and would not leave. Would I make a second 'adoption'? Yes! My passion? The vision? To hear God's praises being sung by Tibetans on the mountains and up and down the valleys of the areas where they live on 'the Roof of the World'.

I am not quick to tell people that I will pray for them. The world is too big. One person cannot give adequate prayer cover to all. My mother's ministry was to pray her family into the Kingdom of God. Until her death in August 2001, I only sporadically prayed for my family. After all, that was Mum's job. My task is to pray only for what He tells me to.

Finishing well?

2001 was a year of loss. My mother had survived a number of serious illnesses and operations, and was doing well. Then came a brain haemorrhage, nineteen days in hospital, and she was gone.

A week after we buried her I was informed that my days in the Netherlands at the missionary training college were numbered to just thirty. Thirteen years living in the land of cheese, bicycles and clogs. Thirteen years of sharing my life with students. And it was over.

Four years before, Dutch immigration had informed me that I would not be able to stay in the Netherlands because of the changing regulations about non-European Union people working in the country. I didn't feel any freedom to pray that this decision should change, because I began to think that God had other plans for me. Other people, however, did pray. Dutch immigration delayed four years, then the blow suddenly fell. Go figure. I couldn't.

That year, everything I touched seemed to be taken away from me. I lost confidence in my ability to make decisions. I became afraid to plan anything. Plans had stopped working for me.

Finishing well? Rather than the question, I prefer the statement. I am determined to finish well. Finish what well? At my funeral service I want it to be said that my life was filled with passion for Jesus right till the end. For that to be said, it needs to be true. I cannot think of much worse than settling down into a boring, lifeless, tepid Christian life; an existence with a 'spiritual' form and yet lacking in lustre, enthusiasm, and sparkle. No way!

And what now? Who am I? What am I? 'Missionary extraordinaire'? Or an ordinary Aussie with a passion for:

Jesus and His purposes for this earth
    and
Vegemite on toast?

Pass the toast.

Jean

While in the last stages of liver cancer, Jean devoted many of her final hours to writing down all that God had done for her. We compiled this story from these notes, plus other personal recollections of Jean.

Finding peace

Early life

'Oh no! Not another one!' The news that she was pregnant again was devastating for Alice Taylor. Her first child was just nine months old. Constantly busy and struggling to make ends meet, she wondered how she would cope. The second child duly arrived, on 31 May 1935, another girl. Named Jean, she grew up as a sickly, skinny child, shy and afraid of anything new.

Because of the outbreak of war Jean could not start school until she was six years old. Many children from the Medway towns and their teachers had been evacuated to safer parts of the country. There were so few teachers left that each class was taught for only one and a half hours a day, sometimes in the air-raid shelter.

Jean loved the informality when only a few children turned up at school. The teacher told them many Bible stories and Jean was enthralled by the beautiful illustrations. Most of all, she loved pictures of Jesus with children. They stirred up a longing to experience His love. She reasoned that if Jesus loved all children, then He must love her, too, but she was frustrated because she could not feel this love and did not know why.

School was not the only place where she heard about Jesus. At the beginning of the war two ladies in uniform went round the streets entertaining the children who sat on the kerb to listen. The women sang happy songs to the accompaniment of a concertina while the children clapped their hands. They encouraged the children to attend Sunday School at a mission hall not far from the Taylors' home. Jean went for a while with some of the other children, but stopped when her mother became worried there might be an air raid while she was away from home.

Growing up, there were times when she asked God for help. Aged 15 and having her her tonsils removed, Jean was terrified at the thought of going into hospital and having an operation. Worse, her period was due on the day she was to be admitted and she had no idea how to cope. She prayed it would be delayed until she got home. Much to her amazement, it was.

Jean was still in her teens when she met Sam Forbes, a charming man six years her senior, who worked in the office of a coal merchant. She fell passionately in love with him and dreamt of an idyllic relationship as his wife.

Sam and Jean were married in church on a sunny September day in 1953. Her father didn't approve and only eleven people attended the wedding. Jean's dreams of happiness lasted no longer than the honeymoon in Devon. As the newly-weds were travelling home the train jerked suddenly while Jean was having a drink. Some of the tea spilt onto her new suit and Sam was furious. He shouted at her in front of the other passengers and told her she was stupid. Cringing with humiliation, Jean felt like a worm and wanted the ground to open up and swallow her.

Jean soon discovered her husband was insanely jealous and insecure. He refused to let her go out to work in case someone looked at her or took her away from him. He also suffered from episodes of terrible depression. Jean suspected these might have been caused by brain damage following a series of major childhood operations; Sam refused help. Jean suffered every kind of abuse from her husband – verbal, physical and sexual – but it was the blasphemous, verbal abuse in public which hurt Jean the most.

They had two children together, Sharon and Brett. In 1968 Sam gave up his office job to buy a working men's cafe in Ramsgate. The work was hard and most days Jean was on her feet for seventeen hours at a stretch, making her hips ache and her knees swell. She hated it, and it poisoned their relationship still more.

After eight years of running the cafe, and twenty-three years of unhappy, bickering marriage, Jean was finished. Reluctantly she gave Sam an ultimatum: he must either seek help for his condition in the next six months or she would leave. He responded furiously and refused to speak to her for a week.

In August 1975, at the end of the six months, Jean walked out. She found work in an office. It was wonderful.

'As I walked the streets everything seemed brighter and greener,' she recalled. 'I was so happy. Things really had changed for the better.'

She was plagued by guilt though. She was the one who had walked out, and he was heavily dependent on her. Ten years later, after another failed relationship, on his sixtieth birthday, Sam committed suicide.

Encounter

Around the time of the separation, Jean had an experience which she kept secret for four years, fearing she would be certified insane if she told anyone about it.

She was cleaning her little flat one Saturday morning when the whole room was suddenly flooded with light. She saw an angel standing in the corner. When he spoke, she was terrified at the sound of his voice even though it was beautiful. The angel had a very brief message for her: 'You tried to be too perfect. There is only one perfect Person and it is not you.' Some years later, Jean read in the Bible about the 'voice as the sound of many waters' and knew she had heard that voice. She concluded the 'angel' was actually Jesus Christ.

Still feeling guilty, Jean started going to church and was eventually confirmed although she had little concept of who God was. She did not see Him as Sovereign, but more as the old man in the sky to whom she prayed when she wanted something.

Having little desire to socialise with other people, especially men, she spent her spare time at home, knitting, sewing, gardening and reading. However, she did start studying for secretarial exams and GCSEs. Night school provided her with a limited social life in a safe environment.

Visions in the night

Then Jean found another social outlet. She joined a group of volunteers who sat with terminally ill people in the evenings and at weekends so their partners could have a break. She felt compassion for these people who sometimes hid their fears from their families but would open up to a stranger.

When the volunteer group sent her on a two-day Bereavement Counselling course, she met Mary who told her she was a Christian. Jean was a bit startled. She reckoned she was a Christian herself, but did not see the need to go round telling other people!

Mary, a widow with two children, told her she knew a lovely Christian hotel where the food was delicious and everyone was made to feel welcome and special. Jean's interest was aroused although she had never heard of a 'Christian hotel' before. Less than two weeks later, Mary rang Jean to ask if she would like to join a church houseparty at the hotel for the weekend. Mary fancied going but wanted a companion. Jean had no idea what a church houseparty was, but the idea of a weekend break just after her forty-ninth birthday was very tempting. She agreed to go. Later she said, 'As we stepped into this lovely place, I felt a wonderful atmosphere of peace. Everything was so tasteful and everyone greeted us as if they already knew us.'

That weekend totally changed her life. After a lovely meal the group met in a huge lounge, making themselves comfortable in the armchairs. Jean felt relaxed as she gazed out of the picture window at the beautiful valley below. It was early June and everything was fresh and green. Her feeling of well-being vanished abruptly when the singing started. Not only did she not know any of the songs, but people started putting their hands in the air. Uneasily she wondered if she had got mixed up with some weird religious sect. Then they started praying – from their armchairs! In a lounge! Jean was horrified. She only prayed on her knees, either in church or in the privacy of her bedroom. How could these people be so irreligious?

However, as she looked around, she was struck by the beautiful expressions on their faces. She wanted what they had. She thought perhaps that if she put her hands in the air she would get the look too. 'I started low down in my lap, then raised my hands slowly, higher and higher, palms outstretched. As I reached the highest point a burning came into my palms, so I thought I had "caught" it.' Afterwards she found the 'real' chapel, knelt down and told God she wanted what the others had.

In one praise session, while singing a modern worship song, Jean was suddenly overwhelmed by the realisation that God was the King who was in charge of everything. The thought that nothing could happen to her without His permission was very comforting; however, during the weekend she often found herself in tears, and this continued after she went home. The burning sensation in her hands continued as well, which made her feel uneasy.

Soon after she got home, her sister Lynn phoned. Jean told her what had happened at the houseparty. She was unaware that Lynn had become a Christian some years earlier. Lynn said, 'I think you have probably been baptised in the Holy Spirit.'

Jean's thoughts about the Holy Spirit were even hazier than her concepts of the Father and the Son. She had heard of the Holy Ghost, but avoided learning more about Him because she did not like ghosts! Kneeling at her bed that night, she prayed, 'Lord, have I really been filled with the Holy Spirit? If I have, why didn't I know about it? And, if this is meant to be such a good thing, why did I feel so miserable when it happened?' Tired, she climbed into bed and fell asleep. She explained what happened next:

'During that night I woke up with the room full of light. Out of the corner of my bedroom was a gently flowing stream of beautiful water. I could see it glistening like a rainbow with silver and gold droplets falling from the flow. It was slowly making its way towards me in my bed. I sat open-mouthed. However, as it got nearer, I began to be afraid. At eight years old I had nearly drowned in a swimming pool and was very afraid of having my head under water. Although I had eventually learned to swim, it was always with my chin stuck up in the air!

'Still sitting up in bed I asked God to take the water away because it was coming over me. He didn't. Instead he took away my fear. I found myself saying, "Come, all come." Then I opened my mouth, my hands, my eyes and even tried opening my ears to receive this beautiful water. It covered me from head to toe on the outside and went inside from head to toe too. It was the most wonderful experience I had ever received.

'For the first time in my life I felt clean and thoroughly washed inside and out. It was so good. I said, "Thank you, God. Now I believe I have been baptised in the Holy Spirit. I can never forget this night."'

She lay down and slept, and had a second dream. 'I was led into a beautiful room, as in a stately home, with a lovely ornate ceiling. Someone whom I could not see was holding my hand. It was an oblong room and there was someone dressed in white at the farther end of it, sitting on a high chair.

'The person holding my hand led me to a series of tall porcelain vessels, each about three feet tall, with lids and gold scroll work around them. Roses and other flowers decorated their square shapes, beautifully delicate and pleasing to the eye. They were lined up in rows of eight or nine. The person holding my hand said, "You can choose." I did not know what I should be choosing, since I could not see the contents of any of the vessels and they were all identical. I was perplexed at first. Then I looked at the person dressed in white and said, "Please can I have the one containing the healing?" I did not know why I said this. The person turned his beautiful face fully in my direction, smiled at me and nodded. That was the end of the dream.'

Afterwards, Jean reckoned that because she had needed so much healing herself, she now wanted to heal others who had suffered in a similar way. The next morning she woke up intensely happy. She knew she had been in God's presence. She had received something no-one could ever take away.

Jean admitted later that, though she had been filled with the Spirit, she knew nothing of the power of the cross, the need for forgiveness or the possibility of having a personal relationship with Jesus. Like many others, she did not think she was a bad person. She was not a thief or a murderer. When confronted by someone who wanted to hurt her, she would not retaliate but just try to keep out of their way.

Three weeks after her night-time vision, while she was praying at home, quite suddenly, she began to realize that although she had done little to hurt others, her thoughts and attitudes towards them had often been wicked. She said, 'I spent a long time repenting that afternoon. I knew I had not lived my life according to God's way and I wanted to change. I suddenly also knew that Jesus was my advocate, my mediator with God.'

As she realised what Christ had done for her, she fell totally in love with Him. She was staggered at His promise never to leave her. 'I needed someone like that. Someone I could trust to stick to me through thick and thin no matter what, even if I did slip up and do wrong.'

She was now keen to meet other Christians who felt like her, but many people in her church seemed to know little of a personal relationship with Jesus. When she spoke to her vicar about it, he encouraged her, acknowledging the reality of her experience and saying he would understand if she decided to leave his church. He suggested that God wanted to use her greatly in His service, but it was not until much later that she fully understood the prophetic nature of his words.

He also lent her a copy of *You are my God* by David Watson. Jean had been impressed by Watson when he appeared on television, thinking he seemed a really nice man. She read his book avidly. When she reached the chapter where he described how he began to speak in tongues, she was totally fascinated and promptly reread it. She wondered if this gift were still available today.

The next day she prayed for the gift of tongues but nothing happened.The following night, she prayed again. Suddenly she felt someone standing behind her. This person took her arms and lifted them in the air. Simultaneously a heavenly language poured out of Jean's mouth. Laughing and crying, she spoke in tongues for several hours. At the end she knew the Lord had brought much healing to her wounded spirit.

Like a child who has suddenly learnt how to whistle, Jean loved using her new prayer language, even though she did not understand much about it. (That simplicity became a characteristic of her life: when in doubt, pray in tongues.) Over the following weeks her prayer language kept bubbling up even when she was in the office, so she developed the habit of disappearing to the toilet to have a little burst of speaking in tongues!

As she read her Bible more, she realised she should tell others about Jesus.The young girls who were her colleagues weren't at all interested. Jean, this middle-aged divorcee, without a partner yet apparently happy, who had been unexpectedly and extravagantly filled with the Holy Spirit but had no coherent English to explain the experience, and who went off to the Ladies to pray in tongues, was hurt and surprised that they thought of her as a complete weirdo! Frustrated, Jean asked the Lord to give her an opportunity to share her faith.

Not long after, the office photocopier broke down. The service engineer repaired the machine and then settled down to eat his lunch while listening to a programme about Egyptian mummies on his radio. He snorted: 'We'll all end up a mound of dust one day!'

Jean jumped, figuring that God had answered her prayer. 'Yes, but that doesn't matter,' she said. 'What matters is whether you know where your spirit is going – to heaven or to hell.'

The man looked at her indignantly and told her she was

speaking rot. At this point Jean realized she didn't have any idea how to explain what she believed in.

Their office was on the first floor. Suddenly there was a noise at the open window. A ladder appeared, followed by the head and shoulders of a window cleaner. 'You'd better believe what she is telling you, chum, because you will have to choose for yourself one day!' The man's T-shirt bore the words 'I love Jesus'. He had overheard them while cleaning the ground-floor windows and could hardly wait to move up and join in the fun. Gratefully, Jean left them to it.

Moving on

An invitation to a wedding led to an unexpected change of direction for Jean. The bride and groom were new Christians, former drug addicts who had been living together. (The groom became a Christian, got baptised in the Holy Spirit, spoke in tongues and got married all within the space of a week's holiday! Jean loved it!)

The wedding was to be held in Ramsgate Register Office and only a dozen people were expected. Jean wore a dress which had suffered rather from hanging in the wardrobe all year. She hid the bumps in the dress by putting a jacket over the top and hoped she wouldn't get too hot during the short ceremony

More than twenty people turned up, all members of a local fellowship which met at Agape House, a Christian hotel in nearby Margate. She also learnt that a surprise reception had been arranged at the hotel.

Jean volunteered to take some of the guests to the reception in her car. They persuaded her to stay, even though she she felt a bit like a gatecrasher because she didn't know anyone except the bride and groom. It was getting hot, and she was feeling more and more awkward and embarrassed.

Then the pastor of Agape House, David Tidy, approached her and began a conversation. Suddenly Jean felt even more ill at ease and tears came to her eyes. 'Do weddings usually make you cry?' David asked.

'No. There's something in you that makes me feel uncomfortable.'

Having heard that David and his wife did counselling, she asked if they would counsel her that day. He told her it was impossible during the wedding, and in any case it was their day off. Jean persisted. Eventually he agreed to give her five minutes if she waited until everyone else had gone.

Impatiently she waited until three o'clock, when the bride and groom left and she was alone with the Tidys.

'Can we pray now?' she asked. They took her upstairs to a peaceful lounge where they prayed briefly. She remembered nothing about the prayer as she was in tears most of the time. David and Pauline recognised the need of more ministry, and invited her to come back the following week. Jean was puzzled: 'Why do I need another session?'

David explained briefly that her history of past abuse had made her vulnerable, not just to human issues like bitterness but to the influence of the demonic, of evil spirits that enjoyed binding people up and destroying them. The uncomfortableness she had felt was these demons struggling in the presence of God who was beginning to act on them. David believed that Christians had authority over demonic forces through Christ so he had told the evil spirits to quieten down and stop troubling Jean. But he hadn't yet got rid of them from her life.

Jean did not understand much of this, but she was impatient for the next session.

The following week David, Pauline and Jean prayed in depth not only about the verbal and sexual abuse from Sam, but also about many things from her childhood. Demons left her. As the tormenting spirits left, Jean felt the Holy Spirit filling the empty areas with grace and joy and purity. It was an exhausting session, but afterwards she felt wonderfully liberated. She decided she wanted to know more about this couple whom God was using in such a significant way.

The Agape House Christian Fellowship became Jean's spiritual home. She was spiritually hungry, aware of her ignorance and age and eager to make up for lost time. She especially loved the prayer meetings. She realized that in prayer Christians needn't just ask, they could exercise authority, in Christ, against evil in the world. Some called it 'spiritual warfare'.

Jean had found her niche. Spiritual warfare came as naturally to her as praising the Lord. She hated Satan for keeping her in bondage all her life and now she wanted to make him pay.

The small hotel had no staff, so Jean began to help with the cleaning on Saturday mornings. Running the hotel was a new project. David and Pauline had only moved in two months earlier believing God wanted it to be like a hospital where people could rest, be healed from bad experiences and learn of Christ's love. They also wanted to hold conferences every couple of months. Jean asked where they were advertising for staff: she was interested. To her amazement they said they were not advertising but asking God to provide the necessary staff. In fact, the help she gave on Saturdays was already an answer to their prayers.

The little fellowship prayed and fasted for help to run the hotel. One day Jean joined them for a twenty-four hour fast. It was her first experience of fasting and something of an ordeal. Not only did she keep thinking about food, she could even smell it! If fasting was always like that, she reckoned she would not do it very often.

The next morning she sensed God saying, 'Do what you know how to do.' She realised He was asking her to give up a good job at the police station and help the Tidys to run the hotel. She would receive no salary and would need to learn to trust God to meet her needs. At the next meeting, she discovered God had spoken to David, too, saying, 'She knows what to do.'

It was already the New Year and the first conference was scheduled for the last week in January 1985. Jean wanted to start work a few days before it began and expected to lose a week's wages because she could not give a full four weeks' notice at the station. However, it was discovered that she was owed one week's holiday, so she left with the same amount of money as if she had worked out the full notice. This small incident was a first proof to Jean of how God would take care of her finances – a reality she enjoyed all the rest of her life.

Not long after moving to Agape House, Jean decided to sell her own home. Her son Brett, now in the army, was buying his own place; Sharon was already married and living away. Jean gave away most of the proceeds. She kept something for her funeral expenses, and put aside another sum to buy a car.

The new car

Jean knew her current car was not going to last long so she started to ask the Lord what kind of car she should get to replace it.

Just at that time, a conference speaker said something to Jean that she received as an answer to her prayer about a new car. This man told her, 'God says you are to lavish on yourself. You have been stingy with yourself all your life. Now He wants you to have pleasure in good things – the best things, which He will provide.'

Jean was astounded, but felt sure this was the Lord's way of telling her how to approach buying her new car. She thought more seriously about what she wanted and mentioned to some of the fellowship that she really only needed a two-seater but did not want a flashy, red sports car with a long bonnet!

'I expect you would like an MGB GT,' said one man.

'Yes,' said Jean, too proud to admit she didn't have a clue what an MGB GT was. She then spent some time wandering around looking at parked cars until she finally spotted an MGB. He was right. It was just what she wanted. She went home and prayed.

Having seen police statistics that suggested silver and white cars had the fewest accidents, Jean asked the Lord if she could have a muted silver one. Then she asked for a few other features:

'I disliked cars with a sunroof, or a folding top. Someone told me that they had stopped making MGBs in 1980. It was now 1985. Therefore I prayed for one of the last ones made. I thought I would never have the money for another car, so it would have to last a long time. The maximum on the clock should be 35,000 miles. Of course it should also be in excellent condition. The last of my house money would be spent on the car, leaving none for extras or repairs.'

Then she thought of something else. The sea air of Margate might make chrome bumpers go rusty, so she added, 'Please, I rather like black bumpers.'

When a visitor to the fellowship, who used to be in the car business, heard her specifications he told her that MGBs had never been made in silver. He suggested she should pray for another colour and get it sprayed. Thinking this would be too expensive, she prayed for a white car instead. It also seemed a good idea to ask the Lord where to look for the car.

The following morning her sister Wendy rang. She had been scanning the motoring section of the local papers and thought she might have found a garage that Jean should try.

Wendy and Pauline both wanted to go with Jean to see how the Lord had answered her detailed request. When they pulled up in front of the garage Jean's mouth dropped open. On the front of the forecourt was an MGB GT, but it was not white. Jean could hardly believe her eyes as she stared at the silver car. 'I glanced through the window just as the salesman came towards us. The mileometer had 35,000 miles on the clock! Again I gasped! One glance showed it had black bumpers and no sun roof. The inside was immaculate – everything I had asked for in a car. God had answered in every detail and more.'

Puzzled about the colour (and just possibly showing off a little) she asked, 'I thought silver MGBs were never made.'

The salesman replied, 'They weren't made as a regular line, but in the last year of production they made fifty silver cars as a limited edition.'

She took it out for a test drive, and soon concluded the deal. When she finished buying, taxing, and insuring the car, she added up the total cost and found that it exactly met the amount of money available. In the six years that she buzzed around in her MG, she never tired of telling people about the lovely way God had provided it.

'I love you'

Jean continued to live at Agape House, hosting their mid-week conferences. During this time she also received a lot of ministry as God dealt with the effects of her earlier life.

By now the team consisted of seven workers, and there could be up to twenty guests.

Much of the ministry consisted of prayer for those in need. About four months after Jean's arrival, David asked her to sit in while he and Pauline counselled people and prayed for them. She sat on one side, quietly praying. David usually asked if she had anything from the Lord, and sometimes she had a significant picture in her mind which showed what the Holy Spirit was doing in that person's life. Eventually she became fully part of the praying team, and she loved it.

The team also took their prayers out onto the streets of the town and outlying areas, especially in areas prone to road accidents or along the cliffs where people jumped to their deaths. Jean claimed the suicide rate went down as a result.

Jean also enjoyed visiting people, telling them how God had mended her broken life, and praying for those who wanted Him to do the same for them. She took part in street evangelism and sometimes, when praying for complete strangers on the streets, she would suggest words or symptoms to them that miraculously gave insight into their lives – a gift she understood to be one of the Holy Spirit's gifts to the church.

Although Jean described Agape House as a safe nest, she realised it was also a place where a lot of her rough edges were being rubbed off. She felt she had become selfish during the seven years she had lived alone and knew God wanted to cleanse her from many wrong attitudes of the past.

It was a fulfilling, happy time, but during it she went through a period of depression that lasted about three months. It began when she asked the Lord to reveal the state of her own heart. When He did so, she wished she had never asked. She imagined that everyone else could see right through her and see how terrible her heart was.

Looking back, she recalled, 'I could barely face people or myself. It was a very difficult time. I could not explain it to anyone, because I felt no one could possibly help me get out of the pit. I was so alone. There was nothing I could do about it, yet I hated the situation. The more I struggled, the deeper I went into the pit. I spent my days off in bed, trying to hide from everyone, yet putting on a joyful mask for the meeting times and for visitors. The group at Agape House were praying for me, but it seemed that I could not pray myself out of the situation. I remember shouting to the Holy Spirit one day, saying "Comforter, why don't you comfort me?" I flung myself upon the Lord.

'Then one day I came across the Scripture "Therefore if anyone is in Christ, he is a new creation; the old has gone, the new has come!" (2 Corinthians 5:17). This hit right into my heart and helped tremendously, because it meant that I would come out of this blackness a new person. The Lord was working on it. The trouble was that I wanted to help Him, but could not. Eventually I did emerge from that black tunnel, and I learned a lot of lessons from it.'

Green pastures

A change of work

Jean fully expected to stay permanently at Agape House. But one day a conference speaker prophesied that God did not want her making beds and doing physical work for the rest of her life. God had far greater plans for her. This was a surprise, and Jean tucked the word away in her mind.

In 1987, she was deeply moved when she saw a video of a Christian doctor working with AIDS patients in London. At the same time, the Ichthus Christian Fellowship was starting a trust to help people with AIDS. Something clicked and Jean felt God was telling her she should become the administrator's secretary. She contacted him and told him what God had said. The man was taken aback! He was not sure he had enough work for her, and was even less sure he could pay her. Jean was not bothered: she was coming and she would find work to do. If there was nothing else to be done, she would read the Bible and pray.

The administrator accepted this determined lady, and Jean prepared to move to London.

Although she appeared very resolute, Jean dreaded living in London and hated the thought of staying in a dark, old house with no garden. But she found a special home with Beryl who became a great friend and confidante. Beryl lived in an Edwardian terrace in a quiet south-east London street, and her garden was beautiful. With fruit trees, squirrels and even a fox, it was better than Jean's garden in the Kent countryside. Jean saw this house and Beryl's friendship as wonderful gifts from God.

The trust ran conferences and visited churches explaining how they could relate to people in their congregations who were HIV-positive or suffering from AIDS. A big house nearby served as an AIDS hospice. Once or twice a week Jean went to help serve meals to the five patients living there. Later she helped prepare special easy-to-eat meals for those suffering from thrush.

Most of the men were homosexual and their conversation tended to revolve around the subject. At first Jean was embarrassed and felt dirty when she left the house. While praying on the way home – she said – she imagined she was pulling slime off herself. Eventually, though, she began to see beyond her disgust. Sometimes she stayed to eat with them and befriend them. She was not a conventional Christian, and her direct approach earned her the men's respect. Surrounded by loving Christians, two of the men gave their lives to the Lord before they died. Eventually the work of the trust was handed over to another agency, but Jean continued doing secretarial work with Ichthus Christian Fellowship (a well-known network of new churches based in south London). She found another outlet in Jesus Action, the arm of Ichthus that helped needy people in the community. Social Services gave them jobs the system was not geared to cover. Tasks varied from cleaning a filthy flat while the elderly resident was in hospital to tackling a pile of ironing every week for a single mother with seven young children.

The unexpected call

In September 1988 Ichthus held a missions day. Jean was totally uninterested and had no intention of going. However, someone was needed to look after the information stand and Jean volunteered. She thought she would join in with the worship time and then do some knitting while everyone went to the seminars. It was not until all the delegates had moved off to the various seminar rooms that Jean realised she had forgotten to bring her knitting!

Boredom drove her to the nearest room. Sitting at the back, she heard about Afghanistan, a country which held no interest for her and whose name she could not spell. She did not know where it was and had certainly never prayed for it.

However, as she heard about persecuted believers, constant warfare, and the urgent need for workers, her conscience was pricked. It seemed as if the Lord were sitting beside her, speaking extremely clearly. 'Yes, and you will be going there one day, too.' This was not an idea she cared to hear. She was fifty-three, and rather preferred the idea of staying behind and praying.

The conference lasted all day. During the evening celebration, Roger Forster, the leader of Ichthus Christian Fellowship, called for those who had been touched by the Lord concerning missions to go to the front for prayer. Jean had no intention of going forward.

'I knew for certain that I did not get up out of my chair,' she recalled. 'I believe the Spirit of God transported me to the front, where Roger immediately clapped his hands on my head and prayed for my missionary call!'

For one week, Jean felt upset and had no peace. 'I was amazed that every Scripture I read was about going out to the nations. I was then reminded about my baptism scripture, Isaiah 60, which begins, "Arise, shine, your light has come." That did it! I asked the Lord's forgiveness and told Him that I loved Him so much that I did not care where I worshipped him, as long as it was according to His will.' Later she told the Lord that she was not going to try to figure out how to serve him in missions, but would simply trust Him to open the right doors.

She joined a prayer group for Muslims at Ichthus and also another group doing part-time outreach to Muslims in London. The team went visiting from house to house one evening a week during the summer months and again each Saturday throughout the year. Every week they met together with other teams to report progress. Of the six who were on Jean's team, four eventually served the Lord abroad.

Short term to Karachi

One Sunday the Ichthus church bulletin carried a small notice: 'Any lady interested in joining a one-month team to work among Afghan women in Pakistan would be welcome. Some medical knowledge would be helpful.' A friend from the Muslim prayer group said to Jean, 'You are praying for Afghans so why don't you go?'

After praying about it, Jean applied for a place on the team. She pointed out that she had no medical qualifications but she had often been involved in medical things, and could pray and engage in spiritual warfare for the team.

So it was that Jean flew out to Karachi in the summer of 1989 and was immediately plunged into a different world. The airport teemed with porters, all dressed in brown overalls and all intent on grabbing her baggage and finding her a taxi driven by a member of their own family.

Besieged by brown overalls, Jean drew herself up as tall as she could and shouted, 'Put my luggage back immediately! I am a daughter of the King on His business, and I don't need a taxi!' The porters quickly hurried away and Jean was left on her own.

She found the free minibus and made her way to the hotel. She was the first to arrive but over the next couple of days the full team assembled. All the others were from America, and most of them were in their early thirties.

Their first trip was to buy local clothes. Jean had arrived with only a summer dress and did not even have slacks to cover her legs. She learned later that she only got away with showing her legs because of her age, grey hair, and the fact that Karachi was a cosmopolitan city. An ordinary dress would have been taboo in the villages, slum areas or in the refugee camp.

The camp where they were working was unregistered because the refugees, some of whom were peddling drugs, did not want to be accountable to the authorities. Most had fled to Karachi in an effort to get jobs or start small businesses. Because the camp was unregistered, the refugees did not receive food or other United Nations' aid.

Jean found the culture very different. She was amused at the way the older Pakistani men used henna on their beards and hair. The sight of them made her want to giggle, but she knew that even looking a man directly in the eye was culturally unacceptable. Whenever she talked to a man she had to get into the habit of directing her gaze over his shoulder.

The men continually chewed betel nut, a mild narcotic, which stained their teeth red. Wherever they spat out the juice the ground, too, was stained red. In some areas, women chewed the nut while at home.

It was an extraordinary month for Jean. 'I had a great initiation into the filth and squalor of the Afghan refugee camp. There was no sanitation. Flies, rubbish and foul smells were everywhere. Meat hanging in shops was totally black with flies, making me shudder inwardly. Children's faces had flies all round them, even on the eyes. My heart went out to them.

'The women were so hospitable and counted it an honour that a foreigner had called on them in their tents. Shoes were always left outside the door. All the neighbours squashed into the tent to see what was happening. The heat was unbearable – we were always soaking wet because of the humidity.

'Various offerings of refreshments appeared before us, and many silent prayers for protection went up as we ate and drank. At one time I was presented with the rare honour of a cup of fermented mare's milk! Usually the drink was green or black tea without milk or sugar, accompanied by small, hard, home-made biscuits or a few toffees served on individual dishes.'

The camp was huge. It included several different ethnic groups, each living in its own community with its own head-man. The team leader spoke a little Uzbek and so was able to communicate directly with the Uzbeks at least.

The team contacted each headman, asking permission to vaccinate the children against childhood diseases. They used school rooms as clinics and worked six days a week doing the vaccinations. One day, when several members of the team were sick, Jean was asked to give polio drops to the children.

Reporting on this experience, Jean said, 'First we found a school room to sit in. When a pile of rush mats was unrolled, two huge cockroaches rushed out. Their backs were so hard it took two men five minutes to squash them with wooden batons. They were filthy, blood-filled things and stank.

'I gave polio drops to about 200 children that day. Most of them wore a little cloth bag around their necks containing a Qur'anic verse for protection. As I dropped the mixture into their mouths, I prayed for them. Whenever I took a very young, sleeping baby from its mother's arms, I would whisper in its ear, "Jesus loves you." I was amazed when the child would startle awake, as if understanding what I had just said.'

Jean had promised the Lord she would go anywhere for Him, and now felt He was saying, 'This is the way, walk in it.'

One day the team leader called her aside. She said she prayed every evening for each team member, using their application form details as a guide. She had seen how good Jean was with the women in the camp, and asked whether she had considered doing the work full-time.

'Not really,' Jean replied, 'but I am praying about it.' The leader told her that when she got home she would send Jean application forms to join WEC International. Jean had never heard of WEC.

Preparation

About a month after Jean returned to England, the application form arrived. She filled it in and sent it back. She was called for an interview two weeks before Christmas. A week after that she was invited to join WEC's four-month Candidate Orientation

Course, starting in January 1990.

The Orientation Course proved to be another learning curve. Initially she thought WECers were very old-fashioned because they often sang from an old hymn book which she had never heard of. On the other hand, she was impressed with how they prayed.

There were fourteen candidates on Jean's course. They learned to get on with one another as they attended lectures in the mornings and did practical work together in the afternoons. Apart from WEC personnel and candidates, there were a number of voluntary helpers living at Bulstrode, mostly foreign students who wanted to improve their English while helping in the house and grounds. Everyone had domestic duties. No-one was exempt. Even the International Director could be seen with his shirt sleeves rolled up, collecting dirty plates from the dining room and loading the dishwasher.

Part way through the course she had a phone call from the Bishop of Karachi whom she had met in Pakistan. 'He was a lovely Spirit-filled man,' Jean said later, 'with a good work going on in his church especially among local drug addicts. Now he wanted to get something going with the Afghan refugees in the camp outside the city. He asked me to return to Karachi to do administration in a school run by the church for local disabled children. This would be a part-time position, giving me a visa and leaving me time to go regularly into the refugee camp.'

At the same time, Di, a nurse from the States was also hoping to work with Afghans in Pakistan. The plan came together that they would set up a primary health care team to visit the refugee camp in Karachi and work with the women.

With just one week to go before leaving the country, Jean needed to sell her beloved MGB. Contrary to the salesman's prediction that the car would sell like a hot cake, no-one wanted it. The bodywork had become rusty from exposure to the sea air and she had neither the time nor finances to get it resprayed.

Eventually an MGB enthusiast expressed interest and came to the house with a suitcase full of cash! However, he started by offering a tiny sum which Jean thought ridiculous. She told him she would rather give it away to a Christian who needed it than sell it so far below its list price. The man then upped the price a bit and asked to take it for a test drive. Back at Jean's home, they continued to discuss the price. Jean mentioned her future work in Pakistan, saying she had hoped the money from the sale would enable her to set up home and keep her for three years. On hearing this, the man upped the price for a third time.

As they continued talking, the word 'immorality' came to Jean, and somehow the conversation got round to what God thought about people who did not live a pure life. At this stage the man looked decidedly uncomfortable.

Her raised his offer for a fourth time and Jean accepted and they concluded the deal over a cup of tea.

Back to Pakistan

Jean stored her possessions in Beryl's loft and said her good-byes. Before she left, one of the elders at the Ichthus Christian Fellowship prayed with her, giving her the promise from Joshua 1:3 that every place where she put her foot, God would give to her. This was a great verse to claim when she started prayer-walking around the city of Karachi! She was also encouraged by Joshua 1:9: 'Have I not commanded you? Be strong and courageous. Do not be terrified; do not be discouraged, for the Lord your God will be with you wherever you go.'

Jean arrived back in Karachi in August 1991. Di was there to meet her but their plans to visit the camp on a regular basis did not work out. Di was working full-time in a local hospital, teaching at the Nurses' School. The work was exhausting. The hospital contributed to the rent of a large house for Di, and Jean was able to move in with her. Unfortunately, it was a long way from the school office and, after some months, Jean found the travelling too tiring in the heat. She was then offered a place in the school compound where she worked. Her companion there was Shirley, a lovely missionary who had been in Karachi for thirty years. She gave Jean lots of tips and orientated her to the culture. They lived in an old colonial-style house which had originally been used by British army personnel.

Jean's room on the first floor shared a balcony with two others but at the end of the rooms there was another large balcony shaded by tall trees. Jean liked going there in the early morning to study and pray. However, she soon discovered it was not wise to sit so near the trees. Green parrots flew squawking between the trees with their tails straight out behind them while huge black kites tried to attack her, and noisy hooded crows dive-bombed the balcony to steal apple cores as soon as she had finished eating.

In November the humidity dropped for a few months, giving cooler nights. Jean enjoyed that time of year when she could sit comfortably in the sun to study, and wear a cardigan in the evenings.

She loved the work in the school office. Most of the teachers called her 'Mrs Jean', but the accountant, who shared her office, could not quite manage this and always referred to her as 'Mrs Jeans'!

After a while, Jean became frustrated at her inability to visit the refugee camp regularly. In fact, she and Di had only managed to get there twice in four months. Remembering that the Lord had brought her there to minister to Afghan women, she prayed about it.

Within a month of that prayer, she was informed that her one-year visa was actually only valid for three months and had now run out so she should apply for another. Every week she went to the visa office, and each time a search revealed that the visa had not arrived. After nine months of this, the authorities told her she must leave the country within seven days because her visa had been refused. The Pakistan Government had just introduced Sharia Law and over forty missionaries had been refused visas.

Jean was dumbfounded, and angry. She said, 'I was willing to pour out my life for these poor people, and it appeared to me that the authorities were stabbing me in the back.' However, she acknowledged that pride could be involved too. 'It seemed I was having to crawl back home without having accomplished the vision of working with the Afghan ladies. I wondered if I would have another chance some time.' A week later, feeling guilty and upset, she returned to England.

Waiting

Beryl was away on a mission in East Africa when Jean returned to England, so it was just as well that she had a spare key to get into the house. One of the Ichthus Missionary Team went round to the house to pray with her, making her feel a lot better. Jean got back involved in her church.

Ichthus was planning a three-week summer mission trip to Central Asia in the dying days of the Soviet Union. Jean put her name down to go, and had an eye-opening time, praying and giving out Bibles in Moscow and in some Central Asian cities that were opening to Christian witness for the first time for centuries: Tashkent, Samarkand, and Bukhara. Jean asked the Lord to give her a room on an upper floor in each hotel so she could pray out over each city.

After the summer outreach, the plan was to join a department of WEC that was moving its office to Cyprus, which was seen as a strategic centre for any opportunities for Christian work in the Middle East and Central Asia. There was as yet no possibility of actually working in Afghanistan.

But six months after leaving Karachi, Jean found a lump in her breast which turned out to be malignant. She was quickly scheduled for surgery and radiotherapy.

Hospital was fine: like the refugee camp, it offered plenty of opportunities to talk with other hurting women. A patient in the ward told Jean that she looked just like a woman who left the previous week. This lady returned to have some stitches out and the patient called across the ward, 'Here she is – the lady who looks just like you.' This 'twin' weighed around fifteen stone, and was black! (Jean weighed perhaps 8 stone and was white.) But when she looked at her face, Jean saw her sister – in Christ. The other patient, not a Christian, had picked up the likeness.

Still Jean wanted to go to Afghanistan, despite the cancer, despite WEC not having any way of getting her there. Having been abused in her marriage, she longed to minister to the Afghan women who had been similarly abused.

She held on to God's promise in Isaiah 35. 'The Lord had said that if I encouraged the feeble and the fainthearted, then He would cause them to be healed and jump for joy. He also said that rivers would spring forth in the wilderness. At this stage I did not know I was going to be working in a desert region in the north of Afghanistan. I did not know when the Lord would carry out His promise, yet I hung on, believing what He said in His word.'

At the end of the radiotherapy Jean was pronounced clear of cancer.

She completed three months in Cyprus in the summer of 1992. When she returned home, she found prospects for working in Afghanistan had finally improved. An organisation which had been engaged in humanitarian aid in the country for over twenty-five years invited other Christian agencies to join the association. WEC became a member during that summer, enabling Jean and another young woman, Bee, to apply.

Before being accepted Jean and Bee had to undergo thorough medical and psychiatric examinations to assess their reaction to stress, in the light of the continuous warfare in Afghanistan. The psychiatrist declared her fit: a testimony, Jean thought, to the counselling and prayer she had received when she became a Christian.

Into Afghanistan

Reaching the goal

It was now April 1993. Before Jean left for Afghanistan, Ichthus asked Jean and Beryl to attend a prayer conference in Pakistan. While there, Jean joined a group who hired a minibus and, accompanied by an armed guard, drove the thirty-six miles through the Khyber Pass to the Afghan border. At the border Jean pushed her foot under the barbed wire onto Afghan soil and prayed for that war-torn country. Excited, she praised God that she would soon be across the border in person.

On the way back, they called on a Pathan family known to some of the group. They prayed with a lady who suffered constant stress headaches. The woman's twenty-four-year-old son had been killed in a blood feud. At some point, her tribe would avenge his death. When they did, the other tribe would quickly retaliate, probably by killing another of her sons. The poor woman lived in constant dread. As the group continued their journey, they saw evidence of these blood feuds – a car riddled with bullets which had recently been abandoned outside a walled village in the Khyber Pass.

After the conference Jean returned to England to make the final preparations for her future ministry. She and Bee eventually left for Afghanistan in July 1993.

On the way they spent a few days in hot, sticky Karachi, staying in Jean's former home. Now she was able to enjoy a leisurely time with her co-workers after the grim experience of having to leave them and Pakistan at short notice. It was like a gift from the Lord. Although unable to visit the Afghan refugee camp, she felt she had finally been able to close a chapter of her life.

Eventually Jean and Bee were informed that their homes in Afghanistan were ready. While Bee had been asked to set up and run a nutrition programme in the Kabul Mother and Child Health clinic, Jean was to become office administrator in Mazar-I-Sharif, a town in the north, about fifty kilometres from the Uzbekistan border.

The ten-hour journey from Peshawar to Kabul started on a fairly good road. Once over the Afghan border, however, the road was all potholes, rutted by years of bombs, rockets and tanks. The minibus and the lorry carrying a load of solar ovens bounced and bumped their way through a dry, desolate landscape of semi-desert hills and small plains. Afghanistan, at last. They passed destroyed and deserted villages and packed, straggling refugee camps.

They wove their way into the valley of the fast-flowing Kabul river, then climbed through the steep, dark gorge to the capital. Set on a high plateau surrounded by mountains, Kabul is 1,800 metres above the distant sea.

Kabul had been bombed and blasted during the conflict with the Mujahidin, and it seemed no-one was rebuilding anything. Not even the rubble in the roads was ever moved – cars simply struggled up and over. The university was blackened and windowless. Many of the students had fled north. All the expatriate houses had sandbags piled against the windows, making the houses dark and cool, even in August.

Two days later, Jean said goodbye to Bee, and travelled 500 kilometres further north to Mazar-I-Sharif with Chris, a British lady, who became a wonderful friend. Chris had been working in Kabul, but was now to be in charge of running the four-month Dari language course for the team newcomers.

Their crowded coach, which had neither air conditioning nor toilet, left the city in the early morning. Jean and Chris sat at the front of the coach and had a grandstand view of the scenery. The road climbed across semi-desert plains, passing by nomads with their sheep and camels, then dropped into fertile valleys with clusters of mud and stone houses perched high on the rocky hillsides above rushing streams. They travelled through spectacular passes of the Hindu Kush, plunged down again into valleys with swollen rivers. They forded streams. High in the mountains, they drove through the Salang Pass tunnel, which had been blasted out by the Russians as a military route from north to south. The approach to the tunnel is covered with sloping concrete roofs to prevent snow or mudslides making it impassable: even so, it is often blocked for a month or two in winter. Potholes and ruts slowed them to a crawl. Mujahidin roadblocks slowed them still more. The driver kept a pile of cash ready on his dashboard and, hardly slowing down, threw bribes out of the window.

Mazar-I-Sharif

Just as they drove into Mazar-I-Sharif, late that afternoon, a white bird swooped in front of the coach. Jean thought it was a dove, a sign from the Lord. Later she learned that the shrine which gave the city its name was surrounded by hundreds of white pigeons. The birds were considered to be *jinns*.

Mazar has been described by one worker as the 'dirtiest, dustiest place you could ever fall in love with.' It is said to have two seasons: the dust season and the mud season. It squats on a flat, semi-desert plain, bounded on the south by a mountain range, and on the north by sandy desert running down to the Amu Darya River – called the Oxus in old literature – now the boundary with Uzbekistan.

Mazar was home to many ethnic groups, but the main language is Dari, a dialect of Persian. In 1980 it had housed only 12,000 people, but by the time Jean left in 1997 the number had swollen to more than a quarter of a million, mostly refugees fleeing the Taliban.

A large provincial centre, Mazar-I-Sharif has four main roads converging on the square surrounding the shrine. A busy bazaar occupies the square and adjacent streets, but other streets are dirt tracks between high mud walls which conceal houses and courtyards. Kiosks and stalls cluster at the roadsides amidst effluent and garbage. Pedestrians, bicycles (often carrying two or three passengers), carts, vehicles, donkeys, camels and sheep jostle for the clearer, less-rutted middle of the road.

Jean and Chris were among eleven new workers joining the three families already living in the city. They were to share a bungalow with Anna, from Finland, who was currently on holiday.

The new team members had four hours of language lessons each day, plus two hours of homework. Jean found language study difficult and struggled to remember what she had been taught. She soon got left behind by the others but did manage to scrape through all her exams. It was a relief when it was over.

The women took turns at cooking. This took much longer than in the West and Jean found food preparation frustrating. Rice, bought in the bazaar, contained husks and tiny stones which had to be removed. In big families, this work and then washing the rice before cooking it takes nearly all day, so for breakfast and lunch many people just ate a flat loaf of bread washed down with tea. Flour and nuts were weevil-infested. The women learnt to spread the flour on a tray and watch the weevils, who hated the sun, find somewhere else to live!

They normally boiled their drinking water for twenty minutes, but Jean preferred to use solar sterilisation, the method recommended by the World Health Organisation for refugees without fuel: put water in transparent bottles and leave them in the sun for at least two hours. The sun's ultra-violet rays kill the germs, even in overcast conditions. Jean tended to play safe, leaving the bottles out all day during the summer and for two days when the weather was dull.

She also learnt how to cook with the solar oven she had bought in Peshawar. It looked like a suitcase with a mirror in the lid. Jean often put two pots of food in the oven before going to the office and then asked the *chowkidar* (house guard) to move it round every hour with the sunlight. She found it excellent for cakes, bread, meat and for slow cooking but useless in winter because of the high courtyard walls.

Huge melons grew locally and Jean loved them. Available from August onwards, they sometimes weighed as much as twelve kilos. Fruit and vegetables were abundant in season and often available dried in the winter. Almonds were plentiful but expensive but dried apricots and mulberries were much cheaper and made excellent snacks.

After a while the three ladies found a woman to do the housework. She had never worked for foreigners before because there were very few expatriates in Mazar-I-Sharif.

She was a pleasant woman, a widow with five children. Jean

discovered she thought herself a nobody. She had no name, she told Jean. Like many other Afghan women, she was referred to as 'the mother of Anis' (her eldest child). Eventually she confided that she was once called Zia Gul. She had suffered abuse before being widowed and she and Jean were able to share their experiences.

Jean had a few opportunities to pray with her – prayer, backed up with love and sympathy, became Jean's main ministry in Afghanistan. Zia Gul told Jean that for years she had endured a pain in her ear. Nothing the doctors had given her had worked. When Jean asked if she could pray in the name of Jesus, Zia Gul agreed. Although she said nothing to Jean at the time, she told the *chowkidar's* wife that the pain went immediately! Another time God touched Zia Gul when she was suffering from severe back pain, but again she said nothing to Jean. When the *chowkidar's* wife told Jean that Zia Gul had diarrhoea, Jean decided not to offer to pray. Eventually Zia Gul asked for prayer herself and again the Lord touched her.

Jean appreciated being able to live with and learn from the other two ladies who already had long experience in the country. Soon, however, she felt confident enough to explore the city on her own and do the shopping. At that time the city was peaceful. If no-one was in sight, Jean laid her hands on the doors in the high walls as she passed, praying for blessing on those who lived inside.

Houses in Afghanistan are typically surrounded by high walls, and the bungalow was no exception. The *chowkidar* answered the gate when people called. He also pumped the well water to the roof tank. He and his family (wife, mother, and unmarried sister) were refugees from Kabul, and lived in two little rooms at the end of the garden. Jean was able to practise speaking Dari with the ladies.

On summer evenings Jean and her companions often sat outside on the step, watching natterjack toads pop out of the grass to hunt bugs for their supper. Easily recognised by the yellow stripe along their backs and their warbling voices which sounded more like bird song than croaking, they bred in the filthy, water-filled ditches alongside the paths. There seemed so many thousands of them in Mazar-I-Sharif that Jean found it hard to think of them as an endangered species.

Their garden had fruit trees and vines, but the ground was

packed mud, as hard as concrete. Jean enjoyed gardening for relaxation and was surprised at the fertility of the sandy soil. She tackled the bare areas with enthusiasm, sowing a lawn and growing vegetables from English seeds. Beetroot, broccoli, and cabbage were unknown in that part of the world, and added variety to their diet. The grape vines were trained onto high poles, but hornets sucked out the flesh from the fruit, leaving dried skins hanging on the vine. To prevent this, each bunch had to be tied into a little muslin bag. It took Jean ages to sew sixty bags to protect the crop!

One evening an ant dropped into her ear while she was picking grapes. The sensation was decidedly unpleasant. 'It was crawling about as if it was wearing boots,' Jean wrote, 'and it seemed to be going deeper. At first I continued picking grapes, but then decided that I should do something about the creature in my ear. Shaking my head did no good. I could feel the ant's struggles getting weaker and weaker, while it went deeper and deeper, and I did not want it to stay inside. Eventually I made a cotton bud and put Vaseline on it. This eventually got the ant out. After that I asked the *chowkidar* or his wife to gather the grapes!'

Temperatures in northern Afghanistan are extreme. In the summer they sometimes reach 50°C. Jean found this was just bearable when the ceiling fans were whirring away, but there was not always electricity to run the fans. Temperatures in January and February could drop to -10°C. Winter proper only lasted about six weeks, but there was plenty of rain to keep the roads muddy and slippery until May.

The shrine

The huge shrine, clad in beautiful blue tiles, which stands right in the centre of Mazar-I-Sharif, is reputed to be the burial place of Mohammed's son-in-law. According to legend, Ali's body was put on a white camel in Saudi Arabia and pushed out into the desert with the idea of building a shrine and a mosque wherever the animal stopped. Although the name Mazar-I-Sharif means 'the shrine of the nobleman,' three other cities also have claims as Ali's tomb.

Pilgrims seek healing there. In March, on Afghanistan's New Year's Day, the tall Jandra pole is erected in the grounds of the shrine. It is said that the first man to touch the pole each year will be healed. Men crowd into the grounds of the shrine, throwing paper money in the air. While Jean was in Mazar-I-Sharif it was reported that a blind man had been healed, yet no one actually saw him or knew him. Jean wondered how a blind man had managed to reach the pole first!

The shrine and the adjacent mosque are a favourite haunt of beggars. Rather than give them cash, Jean opted to give them bread or fruit. On her way to work she would buy a pile of flat bread and hand loaves out as she went. It was not long before some women started waiting for her at the bread stall. They would grab the hot bread out of her hand, tuck it under their *chadors* and immediately ask for more. They didn't show gratitude – perhaps they thought she was gaining merit by giving alms.

Jean was frequently struck by the determination of some of the people. One day she saw a one-legged man walking with a crutch. With his other hand he pushed a bicycle. As she watched, the young man manoeuvred himself onto the bicycle, fixed the crutch behind him, and then launched himself with his one good leg. He kept going by pushing down the same pedal then lifting it. He had probably lost his leg after stepping on a landmine. Mines had been planted for decades, by Russians, the Mujahidin and local factions, and they were still killing and maiming. Ninety per cent of landmine victims are civilians, one third of them children. 50,000 Afghans have lost limbs to them.

Visual impairment is another problem. Afghans often say that Westerners must have weak eyes because most of them wear spectacles, but the truth is that many Afghans have eye problems. For some reason, Uzbeks have the greatest incidence of cataracts in the world. Many Afghans have never had their eyes tested, and are unaware of how poor their sight is. Spectacles are a rare luxury. One time Jean saw an old man wearing diving goggles in the street, presumably because they were magnifying things for him in some way.

Another time, a woman working with blind Afghans was teaching them how to find things dropped on the floor. She said, 'Instead of bending down and feeling around, try shuffling a foot until it makes contact with the object.' At this point someone cheerfully spoke up, 'Teacher, I haven't got any feet!'

God's healing power

Just two weeks after Jean's arrival in Mazar something happened that she remembered ever after.

'I was walking to my language lesson past a group of shop stalls when I saw a young boy, about nine years old, with his foot up on a large dried milk can. I continued walking, but then felt the Lord saying, "I have sent you for this purpose." I retraced my steps to the stall, and saw that the whole of the boy's foot was burnt black, the skin hanging from it in rolls. The boy's face looked grey, and his eyes were glazed with pain. He was in charge of the little shop, as so many young children are, while their fathers go to buy more goods in the city.

'I did not know enough of Dari to ask if I could pray for him, but I remembered the word for "prayer" in Urdu, wondering if it would be the same. I spoke it and made prayer motions with my hands. He seemed to nod his head, so I went ahead and prayed healing over the foot in Jesus' name, hovering my hand over the terrible wound.'

That evening Jean told her friends about the experience, asking them to join her in praying for the lad. Days went by, but she did not see the boy again as she passed the shops on her way to the language school.

Three weeks later, in another part of the city, a young boy approached her.

'I thought he was begging,' she said, 'but he stood in front of me and would not go away. Eventually he rolled up his trouser leg and pointed excitedly to his foot, making prayer motions and pointing to me.

'This was the lad with the terribly burnt foot.

'I looked closely and was amazed to see there was absolutely no sign that the foot had been burnt. The skin was a normal healthy colour, with no pinkness or scar tissue anywhere. The boy then rolled up the other trouser leg and pointed to his other foot. A crowd gathered as he danced excitedly around me. He made me understand that although I had only prayed for one foot, the other one had been burnt too, and was under the shop counter when I first met him. This foot had also been totally healed! I told him that it was God who healed, not me.'

Later Jean returned to the shop and saw both the boy and his father. Now with more fluency in the language, she was able to explain that Jesus had healed the boy. The father seemed to understand and nodded. It was a complete, wonderful healing. Jean was thrilled that despite all her weaknesses, and despite the unclimbed mountains of language and culture, the Lord had still used her to His glory.

Moving house

Language course over, Jean started work in the 'office', a tiny mud-built room with no equipment except a two-way radio on which the team exchanged news with the main office in Kabul every morning. Eventually the organisation rented a house where all their growing projects could have their offices.

Chris returned to Kabul. Jean continued to live with Anna but after a while felt she would prefer to live alone as she wanted more time to spend in quiet intercession. The two women were both in their sixties and having lived with other people for years, the prospect of having their own homes appealed to them.

However, Kate, a worker from Kabul, was due to move to Mazar to establish a Maternal Child Health project and needed to live with someone. She and Jean felt they should live on the same compound, for safety, but have a bungalow each with some kind of connecting room. By the time Kate arrived, God had answered their prayers for the right property: semi-detached bungalows with interior access to a huge cellar which connected both buildings. Again Jean used her spare time to fix up the garden. Her new *chowkidar*, a young man, had never done any gardening before and really enjoyed learning how to coax unfamiliar brassicas from the soil. His family had recently returned from years in Iran as refugees.

The new office

Soon after the new offices had been set up, Jean had to return to the UK for her annual medical check. This also gave her the opportunity to visit prayer groups and share prayer requests. One request was very specific – she wanted the offices to have an inside toilet! The team had run out of funds and the only toilet was a pit latrine 300m away from the office, a long, cold, muddy walk in winter. Jean thought it would be a very poor testimony to have no proper facilities if they were visited by high-ranking Afghans or people from other Non-Governmental Organisations (NGOs).

She never learned where the money came from, but by the time she returned to Mazar-I-Sharif just six weeks later, the house boasted not only a toilet and washbasin, but even a shower!

A succession of Afghans worked in the office. While they were with her, Jean taught a number of them, as well as some English speaking workers from other projects, to touch type. She was also invited several times to speak at an English school run by one of the Afghan project workers.

The team was forbidden to proselytise. Jean never initiated conversations about Jesus. One day a young office worker told her he liked her office because there was always a beautiful smell in it. Jean thought of the sweet aroma of Jesus and quietly rejoiced.

Making friends

As evangelism was forbidden by law, the members of the agency were careful about the way in which they shared God's love. Jean befriended women and prayed for them, waiting for the chance to answer questions about her faith. Some opportunities came about in surprising ways.

One day, as Jean was on her way to the office, a girl came out of a house and told her that her mother would like some of her face cream. Jean explained that she had no face cream and did not dispense medicines. Presuming the mother had some kind of skin complaint, she said she would return as soon as possible to pray with her. When she called that evening she thought the woman looked well but asked what the problem was.

The woman explained that she was not sick, but every time she saw Jean she wanted to look like her. She had come to the conclusion that Jean used a special face cream which somehow lit up her whole face!

Hadija, another friend, was a highly-educated lady with four children. Hadija's first two children had been born in Kabul, delivered by Caesarean section because they were so big. Although the next two babies were born normally, labour had been long and the delivery difficult.

One one visit, Hadija told Jean that she was pregnant again. She was terrified of a difficult delivery and had tried, and failed, to abort the child. Jean could sympathize. Safe Caesarean sections had yet to arrive in Mazar-I-Sharif. The midwife's job was handed down from mother to daughter. Jean had heard of one midwife who had fatally wounded one mother by jumping on her abdomen to speed up a difficult birth. Any baby that somehow survived the trauma of delivery would immediately have its eyes blackened with eyeliner to frighten away any *jinns* (demons).

When Jean told Hadija that God counts abortion as murder, Hadija replied with an Islamic view that abortion was allowed up to three months because the baby is not yet formed. But she was happy for Jean to pray. When Jean added that she should ask forgiveness from the child for attempting to kill it, Hadija readily agreed. The two women prayed together in the name of Jesus. Jean promised she would pray every day until Hadija went into labour, then she would pray continually until the baby was safely delivered. Towards the end of the pregnancy, she prayed specifically for relief from discomfort and for good nights of sleep, and Hadija reported a dramatic improvement!

Jean woke up on Christmas Eve night, knowing her friend had gone into labour. Hadija had found a good midwife living close to her home and early on Christmas morning, after her shortest labour, she gave birth to her smallest baby, a beautiful little boy.

Her husband, a former university lecturer, was not typical of most men in Afghanistan. He was prepared to look after the children and even cook meals when necessary. He was a Muslim, but decided the baby should be called Jesus because he was born on Jesus' birthday. He also wanted the child to know everything about his namesake so that he could choose to become a Christian if he wished!

Although the father had a Bible and asked many questions, he did not reach the place where he wanted to know the Lord personally. However, when Hadija later said, 'I am fed up with Muslims. I want to become a Christian. How can I do that?' he did not stand in her way.

Another time Jean visited a lady whose three-year-old son who had been born with an enlarged liver. After prayer, the child's liver shrank and he was never jaundiced again. His mother, though a Muslim, was quite ready to tell others what the Lord had done for her son.

Every Thursday afternoon Jean kept open house for friends and neighbours and often prayed with people. She also opened her home on Christmas Day. She provided lots of cakes, sweets and nuts for her visitors, but herself spent the day fasting, identifying with the many starving people in the country.

One day, a mother arrived with her three little boys, one of whom had a croupy cough. Suddenly she turned to the other ladies and said, 'I am going to ask Ginaw Jon to pray for my son. When she prays, things happen. Why don't you ask her too?' (The Afghans called Jean 'Ginaw Jon' because they did not like the word 'Jean'. It sounded too much like *'jinn'*, a spirit! They substituted an Afghan name, followed by 'Jon' which is a form of endearment. Jean did not mind the change, thinking it sounded a lot better than 'Jean Jon' would have done!) After prayer in the name of Jesus the child perked up, and the following day he was completely well again.

Not everyone Jean prayed for was healed.

She was warned to stay away from her next-door neighbours because there was a *jinn* in the house. Jean had seen lovely, well-dressed young children coming and going through the iron gate and reckoned there must be a lonely mother behind the high walls. Although she knew no bad spirit was too much for her Father, she did not want to visit alone. Another expatriate, the wife of an eye doctor, agreed to go with her. They fasted and prayed before knocking at the gate.

One of the children answered, then ran to get her mother. Rooya welcomed them into the cool house with Afghan hospitality, providing refreshing green tea along with sweets and nuts. She encouraged her four little ones to shake hands, which they shyly did. Sitting together on a *toshak* (an Afghan mattress), the women chatted.

Rooya said she had a fifteen-year-old son who worked with his father repairing taxis in the city. When Jean's companion asked if there were any other children, Rooya hesitated, then said that her eldest girl was in the other room, but that she was not normal. The visitors asked if they could see the girl and pray for her. Sixteen-year-old Yosamin was deaf and dumb. At the age of twelve she had refused to wear the *chador*, the head-to-toe covering worn by Muslim women outside the home, and consequently she had not been allowed out of the house for four years. She was very frightened when she saw the two strangers and sat with her head bowed, her tousled black hair falling over her eyes.

Jean and her friend prayed for Yosamin as she cowered in the farthest corner of the room, but this was one case where the Lord did not heal, even though Jean continued to pray frequently for the girl. However, as Jean continued to visit, Yosamin got used to her and enjoyed seeing her. Some of this was cupboard love, an opportunity to sneak sweets from the dish while her mother was not looking, but she liked to sit next to Jean and touch her dress or head covering, feeling the material with her grubby hands.

This young girl had nothing going for her in Afghan eyes. She was unmarriageable and was not even able to help her mother in the house. In fact, one of her favourite pastimes was to take wet washing from the line and dress herself in it! Because there was no help for the deaf in that part of the country and Dari sign language was non-existent, she had virtually no means of communication. When her siblings wanted to attract her attention they simply poked her.

An even sadder case was that of Farida who became so severely depressed after the birth of her seventh child that she allowed the baby to starve to death. Farida now refused to leave her bedroom.

When Jean and her companion visited, Farida's old mother and sister had come to help Farida's sixteen-year-old daughter with the cleaning and cooking. They said Farida had a good husband. The sister also had six children, so the yard was teeming with little ones, who all crowded into the small bedroom as the guests were offered the usual green tea. The house, however, had a bad feel about it, perhaps an indication of spiritual oppression. After praying for Farida, Jean and her friend left.

On their third visit Jean's companion encouraged Farida to get up and go outside to the kitchen. She followed them sullenly and began to prepare the evening meal. She heated the oil in a tin bowl and began cutting up onions with a huge knife. Jean was rather worried that she might suddenly use the knife on herself, but nothing happened. When they were leaving, Jean's friend said, 'Tomorrow you must get up and sweep the house!'

The following day Jean bumped into one of Farida's sons and

asked how his mother was. 'She's sweeping the house,' he told her, to Jean's delight. But it didn't last. The next time Jean saw Farida she was sitting outside her gate, rocking to and fro, with a wild look in her eyes. She told Jean not to visit her again.

Girls of all ages were very friendly towards Jean. When they met her on the street they would invite her to their homes to have tea with their mothers. They wanted to know about England and her work in Afghanistan. They could never understand why she chose to work in their country for no wages and presumed she was very rich!

Not all encounters were friendly. Several times little boys threw stones at Jean as she passed by. Fortunately, most missed. When she told her language teacher, the woman was horrified that a respected guest in their country could be treated that way. She suggested grabbing the child by the arm, marching him home and telling his parents. The first time Jean tried this, she turned round only to find the street completely empty! The culprits were hiding down one of the numerous nearby alleyways. The next time, she managed to catch a small boy about four years old. He screamed and yelled so loudly that a crowd began to gather. When Jean explained the problem, one man took the child and cuffed him several times round the ear, making him scream even louder, before letting him go.

Sometimes the outcome was a little more positive. On two occasions the mothers apologised, and asked her in for tea. Another time she caught a boy and dragged him screaming to his house. A tough-looking man came to the big iron door, saying he was too busy to punish the child immediately but would take his belt to him at a more convenient time. 'Please, just tell him that I am his friend,' said Jean. 'And that I will never hurt him.' The boy seemed relieved to be on home ground and rushed into the house. Thereafter, he decided he would prefer to be Jean's friend!

An Afghan journey

Soon after finishing her language study, Jean went to Kyrgyzstan for a conference. She travelled in a team vehicle with two other women who were going on a shopping trip to Termez, just across the Uzbek border, where a market sold a good variety of vegetables as well as chocolate bars and other goodies. One of the office *chowkidars* came along as a male presence.

They crossed the Amu Darya after driving through fifty kilometres of desert. The difference at the border was amazing. On one side of the river ladies were covered from head to foot in *chadors*. On the other side the border was guarded by short-skirted Russian women with bleached hair, clicking along in high heels.

After a good conference, Jean arrived back at Termez. The UN staff helped her cross the border and she asked the UN driver to drop her near where she could get a taxi to Mazar.

She eventually found a minibus whose driver claimed to be Mazar-bound. 'The clock faces on the dashboard had long disappeared, leaving empty, rusty holes, but the very young driver, who looked about sixteen, assured me that we would get to Mazar-I-Sharif without trouble. Then he went up and down the road calling, "Mazar, Mazar, Mazar, Mazar." It seemed I was the only passenger and he needed more travellers to make the journey worthwhile. Eventually, one by one, eight men got into the vehicle.'

Jean asked the driver if they were ready to go. 'Yes, but first I must fill the radiator with water,' he replied. Jean, who had been sitting in the front, had to get out again while he filled the radiator from a bucket of water. She climbed back in.

'Are we ready to go now?'

'Yes, but first I have to get a spare wheel.' He sent a boy off for this, which took a long time as did everything in Afghanistan. At last the spare wheel was in the back of the minibus.

'Are we ready to go now?'

'Of course, but next we have to fill up with petrol.'

Petrol pumps do not exist in Afghanistan. Petrol is sold from five gallon cans beside the road and is measured in a metal cup before being funnelled into the tank. One and a half hours after Jean first got on the bus, it was ready to leave. None of the other passengers seemed bothered by the long wait.

'Have you got a knife?' The driver's unexpected question disturbed Jean. She was a foreigner and the only lady on the minibus. Did the man intend to kill her if she was defenceless? Happily, the only thing he wanted to attack was the melon under her seat! She began to relax, committing the journey to the Lord, and asking Him to get her back to Mazar before nightfall.

Twenty minutes into the ninety-minute journey they had a puncture. All the passengers climbed out and, in true Afghan style, all offered advice simultaneously. One of the other passengers approached her. 'Sister, can you give me some medicine for this?' he asked, pulling his mouth open with a grubby finger. 'This' was a huge, fiery boil on his lower gum.

'I'm not a nurse and I have no medicine, but I could pray for you,' she said. He refused the offer, the only person who did during her whole time in Afghanistan.

Jean spotted another taxi rattling over the sand dunes and jumped into the road trying to flag it down. It did not stop. Meanwhile the tyre was changed, but not, so far as Jean could see, greatly improved. The bus started up again.

'How many dollars do you have?' Again, Jean was suspicious despite the driver's broad grin. She had already taken the precaution of transferring money for the fare to her pocket. The rest was hidden in a belt bag under her long blouse.

'I am English,' she said, 'and we only use pounds in our country.' Dollars were the only acceptable currency in Afghanistan and her evasive answer satisfied the driver. Half an hour later, the spare wheel punctured, so the driver put the first wheel back. As they limped along, he asked for Jean's bottle of drinking water. To her horror he poured the precious liquid out of the window on to the tyre to keep it cool. Then he stopped again.

When another taxi came over the horizon, Jean flagged it down but all the other passengers beat her to it. By the time she caught up, five large men occupied the rear seat, three were sitting in the open boot and two sat on the front passenger seat. The driver did not share Jean's opinion that the taxi was full. He pointed at the front seat. While she squeezed herself into the remaining inches, her bag was put into the hatch-back boot where one of the other passengers used it as a seat. Jean thought sadly of the nice piece of cheese she'd packed on top of her clothes! The crowded taxi pulled away, and they left the driver of the minibus alone beside his stricken vehicle. They finally arrived in Mazar just as dusk was settling on the city.

Unrest in the city

Jean returned to Britain in 1996 for home leave and a check-up. She was delighted when the doctor told her that she need not return home the following year.

Meanwhile the situation in Afghanistan was deteriorating. Taliban forces were closing in on the north of the country and when Jean returned she was aware of heightened tension. One day in May 1997, while returning home from work, she heard gunfire. Hurrying to her house, she sent the day *chowkidar* home. Some time later, Jean heard a frantic hammering at her gate. Instead of going straight home, the man had joined a crowd who were milling around in the street. Suddenly a big gun in the army post, only two doors away from Jean's house, had gone off with a terrific bang. Frightened, the *chowkidar* sought refuge back in the compound. Jean's co-workers were both on holiday, and as the night *chowkidar* had not turned up she was thankful for company.

Jean was not afraid and made the most of the opportunity to tell him why. 'I was very aware that I was in the Lord's hands,' she wrote of this experience. 'After eating our evening meal together, the *chowkidar* slept in my cellar and I went to sleep in my bedroom and slept very well. It seemed that the fighters had decided to sleep, too, because things had quietened down outside.' A day or so later, she listened to a fifteen-hour barrage of gunfire, mostly from the gun near her home. She prayed there would be no incoming rockets. Once the Taliban forces captured the city, things quietened down.

Two days later, when Jean ventured out to the office, she received the normal greetings from shopkeepers as she walked by. Taliban fighters, who came from the Pashtu area in the east, stared at her curiously but were not openly antagonistic. These tall men were quite different from from the local troops. They spoke a different language and wore distinctive black and white chequered turbans with one end hanging down onto a shoulder. Many also wore black eyeliner, which, if the desired effect was to make them look even more fierce, was a bit lost on Jean.

The national workers at the office explained what was happening. The general in charge of the area had fallen out with his second-in-command who immediately offered his troops to the Taliban forces waiting twenty miles outside Mazar. With their combined forces they had overcome the city. But two days later this alliance collapsed into fighting as they couldn't agree how to share the winnings. In the second round of fighting, most of the Taliban were killed. Some escaped. A few were thrown into prison in Mazar-I-Sharif, and the door was locked and not opened again until they had all died of thirst. Injured Taliban lying on the streets were stoned and left to rot in the hot weather; only the Red Cross was willing to bury them.

The team's Regional Manager was concerned because Jean was living alone. One morning, shortly after she arrived at the office, he took her back home to pack a few belongings so that she could stay in one of the houses nearer the office. A jeep was parked outside Jean's compound. This did not worry her unduly because one of her neighbours was a soldier who often parked his jeep nearby.

At the gate, the terrified *chowkidar* told Jean that four soldiers were looting the house. Jean spotted a soldier about to take a can of paraffin from the garden shed. 'That's mine! Put it back and get out!' she shouted. He did!

Jean marched into the house. She found three young soldiers, Kalshnikovs in hand, bullet bands around their shoulders and rocket-propelled-grenade launchers on their backs. They were raiding the cupboard in the hall. Clothes and other items littered the floor. Other cupboards and trunks had been ransacked.

'Get out of my house!' she ordered. 'This is a house of God.' Her Dari vocabulary quickly ran out, so she started at them in her prayer language. One man's eyes widened with fear, then rolled upwards till only the whites were visible. Jean recalled, 'It was like a cartoon, but they said nothing. Then they turned and pushed and shoved to get out of my door together. Getting out in a hurry was not easy, considering their heavy equipment and guns, the narrowness of the door, and the fact they were all trying to get through it at the same time!'

Back in the street, the Regional Manager stopped the soldiers and told them to stay put while he fetched their commander. Two ran off. The third tried to drive the jeep away, but was blocked by the Manager's car.

Jean went up to the man in the jeep. 'Do you make a habit of robbing old ladies who are visitors to your country and are helping your people?' she demanded. 'How would you feel if your own grandmother was robbed?'

Jean saw that the other bungalow had a smashed window. The *chowkidar* told her that it had been repeatedly looted that morning.

Jean took stock of the situation and later wrote: 'The soldiers had taken my computer, radio, cassette recorder, two clocks, my family photograph album and birthday book (because they had pretty covers!), and anything small that could be wrapped into a bundle in my good *chador* which they found hanging in the hall. My good walking shoes had been stolen, so had my brand-new flip-flops, and also half a bottle of perfume. The one who had taken my flip-flops had left his old broken ones behind. For days I checked soldiers' feet as I walked to work to find out if they were wearing a pair of new flip-flops with 'Pansy' written on the side.' She wondered what she would do if she found the thief, and hoped she would have the grace to ask God to bless him.

Feeling her home had been polluted by the looters, she went through each room praying and rededicating it to the Lord and His work.

Jean was glad when the Red Cross plane began operating again, allowing her to fly out of the country. She went to Mussoorie, in the mountains of North India, travelling with a friend from Peshawar. 'It was so good to get out of the heat and dust of Mazar-I-Sharif,' she said, 'and to walk among green trees and enjoy the lovely fresh air of the Mussoorie mountainside. The place where I stayed with a WEC couple was peaceful, and I enjoyed their fellowship.'

In India she also managed to replace her stolen goods. People also gave her gifts, even a replacement computer. When she returned to Mazar at the beginning of July, the city was almost back to normal, but with a slight sense of unease. The general who had kept the peace for ten years had fled to Uzbekistan. An Uzbek himself, he was apparently among the last group of people to be allowed to across the border at Termez.

Another enemy

That summer was long and hot, and the continuing lack of electricity made it almost unbearable. In August, Jean fell ill. The symptoms seemed to indicate amoebic dysentery so she took a ten-day course of treatment. She had had dysentery before and knew she could expect side effects from the medication: dry mouth, nausea, general discomfort and so much fatigue that she would want to sleep all day. Last time the side effects had lasted for a month. This time, however, symptoms went on and on.

When she returned to the office, she conserved her energy by resting during her lunch hour and taking a taxi rather than walking.

One day in early September the sudden sound of gunfire prompted a hasty end to her day's work. Jean, Kate, Delia and Margaret used the project vehicle to get home. From time to time they heard shots being fired from the big gun in the army post. Thankfully there was no return of fire which might have hit their houses.

At 7.30 p.m. the women heard noises in the compound. They knew it could not be the night *chowkidar* because the shooting made the streets too dangerous for him to get to work. While Kate and Margaret prayed in the cellar, Jean and Delia went to investigate. Four men had stood on each others' shoulders to climb over the compound wall.

Speaking a dialect Jean did not understand, one man put his gun to her stomach and took the safety catch off. Guessing he meant her to go indoors, she moved quickly. At the same time she prayed for protection for herself and her companions.

While three men stayed upstairs, the fourth led the women back into the cellar. He demanded dollars but they told him their money had already been stolen. When he ordered them to give him the car and gate keys, they handed them over. They declined to mention they had already disabled the car.

The cellar room was lit by a paraffin lamp. The glass chimney had broken and because they did not have the correct size to replace it the ladies had balanced a larger glass on it, which leaned at a crazy angle. Before joining his mates, the robber tried unsuccessfully to straighten the glass, then warned the women to be careful the lamp did not fall over and start a fire! A few minutes later they heard the men trying and failing to start the car. Then they left, saying they would return the following day with a mechanic.

Feeling extremely vulnerable, the women took turns watching for intruders. At 2.30 a.m. the dog next door began to bark. Delia woke Jean with the news that two more intruders were trying to get in. They decided to frighten them off by banging saucepan lids together like cymbals. It worked! The thieves had probably thought the house belonged to UN workers who move away during disturbances.

The next day the team heard the noise of aircraft, and then the crump of bombs falling. They learnt later that no-one was injured because the bombs were so old only one had exploded and it had fallen on an empty house.

Delia and Kate needed to visit the office on the second day, so Margaret stayed at home with Jean who felt too weak to go to work. In the middle of the day, Margaret spotted men climbing over the wall. The women retreated to the cellar and prayed, asking the Lord what to do. They both felt they should remain absolutely silent if they were found. They heard two men trying to start the car again, and others ransacking Kate and Delia's house.

Twenty minutes later they heard footsteps on the cellar stairs. A black-haired Afghan carrying a Kalashnikov popped his head round the door and looked at them in surprise. He sped back upstairs and the women heard mumbled voices. Another man came down and greeted the women. They kept silent. He assured them he would not hurt them, but they still said nothing. Finally he went back upstairs. The soldiers still could not start the car, and the last the women heard was them pushing it out of the compound.

The offices were looted and a total of six cars stolen. Fortunately, the thieves did not take the computers and were unable to break into the main safe. They did, however, open a smaller safe in Jean's office and took everything they could, leaving papers strewn everywhere. They stole the generator and wrenched the electric fans off the walls.

Overwhelming peace

Medical emergency

When the fighting quietened down, the Red Cross made a plane available for expatriates wanting to leave Mazar-I-Sharif. All the organisation's families left plus some singles who were due for home leave. By the time the plane had made two trips to Pakistan, just seven workers remained. Jean had reckoned the flights would be crowded and, although sick, had opted to stay because she was familiar with running the office and the radio system.

Her health, however, showed no sign of improving and it was

not long before the team nurse called one of the two remaining expatriate doctors to examine her. Thinking an amoeba might have made its way to Jean's liver, the doctor referred her to a hospital in Islamabad where he said she would be well looked after. Jean managed to send an e-mail to WEC in the UK, telling them about her condition. The reply was quick: 'Because of your past history, get back to UK if you possibly can for treatment.' She was surprised. She had not thought of cancer.

Making travel arrangements by radio through friends in Pakistan was always difficult. It was nightmarish now, with Taliban planes sporadically bombing the city. Jean was too weary to handle it so she prayed, asking the Lord to arrange everything.

The doctor put in an urgent request for a plane to fly her to Pakistan. There was no guarantee when it would be safe for a plane to land, so Jean had to be ready at any time. She later recalled, 'I could hardly think what I needed to pack. It was early October and would probably be cold in the UK. Opening my suitcase, I lay on the bed thinking. Next time I got up, I virtually threw in the items I thought I would need, then went back to bed. I did not know I would never see that house, garden, or those remaining possessions again.'

She waited like this for nine days until the plane came, The team nurse and her husband accompanied Jean to Islamabad, leaving just two ladies and one man of the small team left in the city.

The only way Jean could travel the eight bumpy miles to the airport was strapped to a to a canvas stretcher in the back of a van. She felt sick on the flight to Kabul and a very bumpy landing proved to be the last straw. Jean was so grateful to the nurse for sitting beside her throughout the journey.

They changed to a Red Cross plane going to Peshawar. The British High Commission in Islamabad had arranged for the plane to continue on to Islamabad, saving her a four-hour journey over a rough road. Jean was grateful, not only to the British High Commission, but also to the Red Cross team who put themselves out by flying those extra miles.

Jean was met in Islamabad by the Director of British Airways in Pakistan, a smart young British man. He told her she would be leaving for the UK at 9.30 the following morning, accompanied by a nurse who had been working in Peshawar and needed a break. Jean then discovered that the nurse who would be accompanying her was none other than Doris, a good friend from her church in London. Having organised all the flight details, the BA Director saw Jean settled in a clean local hospital for the night. By this time her nausea had worn off and she was ravenously hungry. The kind BA director promptly went home, returning half an hour later with two home-made sandwiches. Next morning, after food and rest, she began to feel better. At the airport Jean stayed on a stretcher in the ambulance until Doris had checked in her baggage. Eventually they loaded her into the plane via the hatch for the food trolleys. Six seats had been converted into a bed. Although not actually in pain, Jean could only lie on one side because the other was so tender and uncomfortable. The eight-hour journey seemed endless. In between snatches of sleep she totted up the number of stretchers used during the trip: 12.

Home in England

An ambulance was waiting at Gatwick Airport to take Jean and Doris to Bromley Hospital in Kent. Jean wondered why Bromley Hospital had been chosen, then realised that one of the consultants there was Steff, the head of her church mission team who had been responsible for liaison between the Ichthus church and the organisation in Afghanistan. Jean was thrilled at the Lord's goodness. She had committed the journey to Him and now she was home without having had to do anything.

For a week Jean underwent various tests and then saw the oncologist, an attractive lady who gently told her she had cancer of the liver and could only expect to live for a matter of months. When asked if she would like chemotherapy, Jean's immediate response was negative. She felt tired rather than ill, and everything she had heard about chemotherapy was bad. The thought of frequently feeling ill to gain a short extension of life did not appeal.

Jean was not shocked by the diagnosis and believed the Lord had prepared her to hear it. What she most wanted now was rest and a peaceful environment to recover from the events of recent weeks. She was exhausted from the journey, and from the trauma of war, and robbery and of being threatened at point-blank range with a cocked gun.

She said, 'It is not until you leave the place of trauma that you realise how it has actually affected you. Had I been well, I would have carried on working in Mazar-I-Sharif as normal. I had felt so spiritually dry in Mazar-I-Sharif that I was crying out to see more of Jesus in my life, even though He was using me in various healing situations. I wondered if He was about to take me to heaven to be with Him, so I could spend all my time in His presence. I liked that idea.'

Jean's former pastor, David, came to visit, along with his wife. He wanted to know if Jean was praying for healing. He mentioned that some members of his fellowship were, but felt they should not continue do so if she was not seeking healing herself. Jean, in fact, hardly had the energy to pray at all. Her prayers for herself had been restricted to asking the Lord whether her illness was the result of sin. Nothing had come to mind except the story of the blind man in John chapter nine where the crowds had wanted to blame the man's blindness on sin. She recalled Jesus' answer: 'Neither this man nor his parents sinned, but this happened so that the work of God might be displayed in his life.' These words were enormously comforting.

During her two weeks in Bromley Hospital she had some lovely opportunities to speak to fellow patients about the Lord. They were amazed that she could be so calm after being told she would soon be dead!

Embracing life

Jean began to have second thoughts about simply accepting an early death as inevitable. After all, she was only sixty-two and nowhere near the three-score years and ten promised by the Lord! And what if He had brought her home in this dramatic way to prepare her for a new ministry? She began fighting. Her appetite returned and she grew stronger.

When she asked the Lord for encouragement, she saw in her mind's eye a garden containing a rose bed set in a lawn. Describing the picture, Jean said, 'The patch contained rose bushes all round the edge, but right in the centre was a much taller, beautiful rose bush. All had lovely flowers on them. God showed me I was that tall bush. My perfume was lovely, and there was so much that it spread over all the other bushes and covered them too.'

Such was the effect of her life of intercession. It was a holy moment. Jean realised how special she was to Jesus – and at the same moment, felt sorry for other Christians who failed to realise that they, too, were special to Him.

Choosing to live was as much a spiritual battle as a physical and mental one. One night in hospital, Jean had an unwelcome visitor – the devil. Later she recorded that 'He stood silently, a tall man dressed in black, beside my bed. I told him to go because I belonged to Jesus and had no business with him. He left my bed but I was aware of him standing near the window. I went back to sleep, but then he was beside me again, carrying a black blanket and with a nurse I had not seen before. He said I must be cold, and told me the nurse said he was to put the blanket over me. I suspected he wanted to smother me. It was quite warm in the ward, so I told him I was hot and did not need a blanket. I told him to go away in the name of Jesus, because I loved Jesus and belonged to Him. The devil disappeared and I never saw him again.'

Other visitors were much more welcome! Among them was her son Brett. Although he was somewhat reassured when she said she was up and about, he took three days compassionate leave to visit her.

Finding a home

Jean now faced a dilemma. Her friends in the London church wanted her to stay in the Bromley area so they could visit, but her daughter Sharon could only get to Bromley once a week and wanted to be near her mother. Although Jean felt she was letting down her London church, who had done so much for her, she wanted to be near Sharon, because she had spent so little time with her in the years since she had become a missionary.

The first step was to change hospitals. She was transferred by ambulance to Margate Hospital where she spent a further two weeks and was visited every day by Sharon and her husband Richard. She was still very tired, and her badly swollen liver interfered with deep breathing. Catching a cold revealed just how shallow her respiration was. When she wanted to sneeze she could not draw in sufficient breath, and coughing left her aching and breathless. Although she was in no pain, the swelling prevented her from bending over. She was most comfortable lying flat.

At Margate an oncologist and a Macmillan nurse took time to discuss chemotherapy with her, explaining exactly how it worked and what progress had been made in the last few years. Side effects could be minor and quality of life greater. Although the cancer could not be cured, they told her that she should not need to spend all her remaining time in bed. When Jean mentioned that she wanted to write her autobiography, the doctor asked, 'How can you type while horizontal? At least we should be able to have you sitting up comfortably.' He reckoned she should be able to live normally – walking, shopping and working. This was hard for Jean to imagine, but she said she would think about it. What the doctor had said certainly made sense.

A place was booked in the local hospice for when she would need it, but in the short term Jean was homeless. Although it was suggested that Social Services could provide a flat with back-up services, Jean she knew she was too weak to look after herself. Sharon did not have enough room for her to live with her family, so she investigated local nursing homes and found an excellent one in nearby Westgate. When Jean saw it she was delighted. It was only fifteen minutes from the beach and the sea air smelled so good after the dryness of land-locked Afghanistan. Even the screeching seagulls made a welcome sound.

The staff were friendly and Jean soon settled in to her room with its en-suite bathroom. Unlike many of the patients, Jean could bathe, dress and feed herself, although she could not yet bend over to tie her shoes or wipe the bath after using it. The matron lent Jean her new office chair so she could use her computer, but she only had the strength to work on her book for half an hour a day. Then, exhausted, she would spent most of the time lying down.

A Macmillan nurse, who visited weekly, realised that much of Jean's exhaustion was due to lack of air. Jean's lung space was restricted both by her swollen liver and by fluid. On the nurse's recommendation, Jean saw a physiotherapist who showed her how to take in more oxygen, slowly practising breathing up to a count of six or more. It worked! Her quality of life changed dramatically as she got more energy. She had been exercising by climbing the stairs. Initially, this had involved resting three times between the ground floor and the first floor where her room was. After one week of deeper breathing, she could do it without stopping, a great breakthrough. It also doubled the amount of time she could spend on her autobiography.

Chemotherapy started in December 1997. She was pleased to learn that her particular treatment would not make her hair drop out. There were ten other possible side effects. Friends wrote to say they were praying that these wouldn't happen. To a large extent, none did.

She responded very well to the therapy. By the end of the final session, her liver was back to its normal size. When the specialist expressed surprise at how fast her liver had shrunk, Jean made the most of the opportunity and told the doctor it was because God was in charge!

She felt much better, looked good and was delighted that her clothes fitted properly now her waist had shrunk! She had more energy and her quality of life improved. She started going for short walks to the nearest shops or to post a letter. This was another big breakthrough – only three months earlier Sharon and Richard had been pushing her in a wheelchair for some sea air and a change of scenery.

At this time Jean appreciated having contact with her friends from Agape House. 'I was only two miles from my original church fellowship which now met in a community hall,' she wrote. 'Agape House had been sold some years before. One church member had to pass my door, and she picked me up each Sunday from the nursing home. The church members put chairs together so that I could lie down and they were very comfortable! I am ashamed to say that the first time I went to church I fell asleep while the pastor was speaking. The pastor and his wife visited me regularly, both in the nursing home and while I was having my chemotherapy sessions in hospital. A friend from the church visited me weekly to share the mid-week Bible Study and pray with me.'

Many of the people in the nursing home had lost their independence very suddenly following a fall or stroke. Jean wrote, 'God is being glorified in the nursing home as I speak to individual ladies who are depressed. It is hard for them to end up in a nursing home without being prepared beforehand for disposing of their homes and all the memorabilia of a lifetime. I was so glad I had sold my home fourteen years before and had none of this trauma.'

As in Bromley, Jean had opportunity to speak to other patients during her visits to Margate Hospital. 'Ladies recognised my peace and sometimes asked how I got like this, whereas nothing seemed to stem their own panic attacks. Of course I am always ready and able to speak of the Prince of Peace and pray with those who are willing. On every occasion we must lift up the Name of Jesus, because the end is very near and He wants no-one to be lost.'

And last

Jean longed to be more independent and mobile, so she explored the possibility of driving again. Ichthus Motor Mission provided her with a car, enabling her to visit family, friends, and church. In June she managed a cross-country drive to the annual WEC prayer conference in Devon, where she shared briefly. At the end of August she went to another holiday conference, this time in Sussex with Ichthus. These holidays gave her the chance to catch up with old friends, and to enjoy the rural scenery in Dartmoor and the country grounds laid out by Capability Brown in Sussex. Only a few close friends realised that she was once again becoming breathless. Next she spent a week with Beryl at her old home in London.

Jean ignored the symptoms of returning cancer. In the middle of September she sent WEC the draft of her autobiography. By the end of the month she was in the hospice for respite care, but further tests indicated that no further treatment was possible. She returned to the nursing home, becoming progressively weaker but suffering no pain.

In the middle of November she asked to return to the hospice. As the end approached, she was unable to speak but still acknowledged visitors with a gentle squeeze of her hand. One commented that instead of anointing for burial it was more like anointing for resurrection!

On 18 November 1998, just four days after going into the hospice, this 'intrepid lady who gave the later years of her life in intercession and service' went to join the Lord she had grown to love so dearly.

Jean's passion for people to come to know her Lord never ceased. Her autobiography ended with an invitation:

Jesus, the Son of God, says, 'Peace I leave with you; my peace

I give you.'

If He says it, it must be true. How? We can have peace in Jesus when we give our lives to Him. He knows exactly what we are going through. We can never go through greater tribulations than He endured for us when He was humiliated, beaten, and crucified.

To accept Jesus into your life is called being born again (John 3:3-7).

You can start a new life now by saying the following prayer and meaning it in your heart:

'Dear Lord Jesus, I believe that You are the Son of God, that You died on the cross for my sins, and You love me. Please forgive my sins and wash me clean. Help me now to follow Your example and grow more like You, to love and obey You forever.'

*Some centres from which you can find out more about
the work of WEC International*

Web and email

www.wec-int.org

Mail and phone

Australia
WEC International 48 Woodside Avenue, Strathfield, NSW 2135,
Australia
Phone (0)2 9747 5577

Brazil
Rua Carlos Monte Verde 25, Boa Vista, 31060-350 Belo Horizonte, Minas
Gerais, Brazil, S America
Phone (0)313 488 1118

Canada
WEC International, 37 Aberdeen Avenue, Hamilton, ON L8P 2N6,
Canada
Phone 905 529 0166

China (Hong Kong)
WEC International, PO Box 73261, Kowloon Central Post Office,
Kowloon, Hong Kong
Phone 2388 2842

France
AEM-WEC (Action d'Evangélisation Mondiale), 27, rue de Mulhouse, FR-
68110 Illzach, France
Phone (0)3 89 504580

Germany
WEC (Germany), Hof Häusel 4 D-65817 Eppstein, Germany
Phone (0)6198 9005

Korea
Seo-Cho PO Box 137, Seoul 137-601, Korea
Phone (0)2 529 4552

The Netherlands
WEC, Waalstraat 40, NL-8303 DH Emmeloord, The Netherlands
Phone (0)527 616 521

New Zealand
PO Box 12033, Hamilton, New Zealand
Phone (0)7 824 3211

Singapore
WEC International, 5 Jalan Bangket, Singapore 588950
Phone 6463 3891

South Africa
WEC International, PO Box 47777, Greyville 4023, South Africa
Phone (0)31 303 2533

Switzerland
WEC International, Falkenstrasse 10, CH-8630 Rüti, Switzerland
Phone (0)55 251 5273

Taiwan
P.O. Box 7-261, Taipei 106, Taiwan, R.O.C.
Phone (0)2 291 44960

United Kingdom
WEC International, Bulstrode, Oxford Road, Gerrards Cross, Bucks. SL9
8SZ, UK
Phone (0)1753 278103

USA
PO Box 1707, Fort Washington, PA 19034 USA
Phone 215 646 2322